HD
6509
.R4
B3
1983

Barn

**Walter Reuther
and the rise of
the auto workers**

John Barnard

Walter Reuther

and the

Rise of the Auto Workers

Edited by Oscar Handlin

Little, Brown and Company · *Boston* · *Toronto*

Library of Congress Cataloging in Publication Data

Barnard, John, 1932–
  Walter Reuther and the rise of the auto workers.

  (Library of American biography)
  Bibliography: p.
  1. Reuther, Walter Philip, 1907–1970. 2. Trade-
unions—United States—Officials and employees—
Biography. 3. International Union, United Automobile, Aerospace, and Agricultural Implement Workers
of America—History. I. Title. II. Series.
HD6509.R4B3   1983   331.88'1292'0924   [B]   82-14894
ISBN 0-316-08142-6

LIBRARY OF CONGRESS CATALOG CARD NO. 82-14894

ALP

Published simultaneously in Canada
by Little, Brown & Company (Canada) Limited

Printed in the United States of America

The author wishes to thank *The New York Times* for permission to use copyrighted
material, as follows: on page 50, headline from January 24, 1937; on page 102,
extract from September 17, 1945; on page 187, quotations of Walter Reuther
from March 29, 1964 and April 14, 1966; on page 188, quotation of Walter
Reuther from October 14, 1966; on pages 190 and 191, extracts from June 14,
1966; on page 191, extract from June 17, 1966; on page 191, quotation of Walter
Reuther from August 27, 1966; on page 192, quotation of Joe Curran and
George Meany from November 15, 1966; on page 200, quotation of Walter
Reuther from December 2, 1969; on page 210, extract from May 12, 1968; on
pages 213 and 214, extracts from May 11, 1970. All extracts copyright © in the
year indicated by The New York Times Company. Reprinted by permission.

The author also wishes to thank Houghton Mifflin Company for permission to use copyrighted material appearing on pages 4, 7, 8, 10, 14, 15, 16, 42, 43–44, 60, 66, and 129 of this volume. These extracts are from *The Brothers Reuther* by Victor Reuther. Copyright © 1976 by Victor G. Reuther. Reprinted by permission of Houghton Mifflin Company.

Editor's Preface

THE AMERICAN LABOR movement entered the decade of the 1930s singularly unprepared for the Great Depression. Union membership had been declining for a decade, and large sectors of the working population remained totally unorganized.

Industrialization had long created difficulties for wage earners in the United States. But when the drive toward organization had developed early in the twentieth century, it had focused instead primarily on the craft unions. In the railroad brotherhoods, the building trades, and some branches of tailoring, skilled workers relatively few in numbers had the bargaining power to protect themselves. However, they stood largely apart from the great new industries that expanded rapidly after the First World War—aluminum, steel, chemicals, and electrical products. These modern factories were singularly inappropriate places for craft organizations. They employed a few skilled workers, but the major part of their labor force consisted of unskilled day laborers who received low wages and suffered from high rates of turnover and frequent seasonal unemployment.

Most important of these new industries was the manufacture of automobiles—modern, highly mechanized, and concentrated in a few great enterprises. Other than the empire built by the eccentric individualist Henry Ford, the automobile firms were controlled by great corporations, with General Motors the largest of them all. And all producers resisted unionization with every means at their disposal. Only an industry-wide labor organization could cope with such formidable antagonists.

Furthermore, the old labor unions were not prepared to approach these massive corporations. On the one hand, they suffered from the depredations of racketeers who operated at their fringes; on the other, they were sometimes victims of radicals interested less in the welfare of the workers than in seizing the unions as a means of effecting social change.

Yet in these unpromising circumstances Walter Reuther participated in the transformation of an important sector of the American labor movement. He played a prominent part in the organization of the United Automobile Workers in 1935, and, in the following decade, fought in the bitter factional struggles that shaped the future course of that organization. He finally became president in 1946, and from that position he enunciated advanced concepts of the place of labor organization in the modern economy. Professor Barnard's study traces these developments through the biography of a colorful and thoughtful man.

OSCAR HANDLIN

Acknowledgments

MY GREATEST DEBT is to the many who make available to scholars the resources of the Archives of Labor History and Urban Affairs at Wayne State University. Preeminent among them is the United Automobile, Aerospace, and Agricultural Implement Workers.

I am indebted to Oakland University for a sabbatical leave in 1979–1980 and to its Research Committee for a grant in 1974 and a fellowship in the spring of 1978.

Gilbert Gall and Stephen B. Barnard, two students of history, assisted in portions of the research. Patricia A. Tucker, Judy Langdon, and Anne H. Lalas typed the manuscript, which was read by David Burner, Warner Pflug, and Seth Wigderson. I am grateful to these generous friends for their help and their kind corrections of my errors. Those that remain are my responsibility alone. Marian Ferguson, Katy Carlone, and Madelyn Leopold, my editors at Little, Brown, were unfailingly helpful and enthusiastic.

Finally, I would like to thank those brothers and sisters of the Oakland University chapter of the American Association of University Professors who looked after our union while I was writing this book.

Contents

Walter Reuther

and the

Rise of the Auto Workers

I

Preparation

A FAMILY HERITAGE directed Walter P. Reuther to his
life's work. His German immigrant father, Valentine Reuther, a
fervent unionist and socialist, reared his sons in the conviction
that a democratic social commonwealth would ultimately replace capitalism. The parents gave their son love as well as
lasting moral and intellectual perspectives, and thereby shaped a
character eagerly active, ready to confront and conquer society's
ills and evils, and stubbornly self-confident. Reuther entered
Detroit's automobile factories only a few years before the Great
Depression laid bare the faults in America's economic system.
With his father's teachings on capitalism's injustices and waste
thus confirmed, he enlisted for life in the cause of the auto
workers' union.

The industrial union of Reuther's maturity emerged in
response to the economic predominance of giant corporations
in most of the nation's basic industries. By 1907, when Reuther
was born, the United States led the industrial world. A torrent of
goods flowed from its factories, mines, and shops. Although
automobiles had only recently appeared on American roads,
their manufacture would soon require huge, ingenious factories
and hundreds of thousands of workers. In Detroit, Henry Ford,
after years of experimentation, prepared to launch his Model T,
a simple car for the common man. Ford's assembly line
methods of production would lay the foundations of an industrial empire and a fortune, and transform the working lives
of millions. Reuther's life began as the modern factory with its
novel processes, unique stresses, and productive abundance
came into existence.

On September 1, 1907, Labor Day eve, Walter Reuther was born in Wheeling, West Virginia, a city of iron and steel mills, glassworks, and riverboat shipyards, with a population of 40,000. German, Polish, Scandinavian, Slavic, and Irish workers, along with the native born, crowded the steep streets and clangorous factories. Wheeling's work force was effectively organized for that time in over forty local labor unions, whose membership reached nearly 4,000.

Reuther's parents formed part of the immigrant throng. Valentine Reuther was born in the Rhineland village of Edigheim, arrived in the United States in 1892 at the age of eleven, and settled with his family on a farm near Effingham in southern Illinois. A few years later he joined relatives in Wheeling, went from job to job for a time, and married. At Walter's birth, he drove a delivery wagon for the Schmulback Brewing Company. Energetic, friendly, and articulate in both English and German, he rapidly gained the confidence of his fellow workers. A founding member of a United Brewery Workers local, he was elected the union's delegate to a local labor federation, the Ohio Valley Trades and Labor Assembly, and became the assembly's president at the age of twenty-three. Reuther's mother, Anna Stocker, was the daughter of a German wagon maker in Scharnhausen, near Stuttgart. She arrived in Wheeling in 1902. The couple met in a Wheeling workingman's saloon where Val delivered the beer and Anna worked in the kitchen.

The German village life of Reuther's parents had revolved around family, work, and church. They were poor people whose children worked in the fields and at home from an early age. Both families were Lutheran; but Val Reuther's father, Jacob, who brought the family to the United States, was a dissenter who charged that the Lutheran church and clergy neglected ordinary human needs. He was also a pacifist who recalled the horrors of war in the disputed Rhineland. Although Anna's family was more conventional, she was a woman of independent spirit, who left for America when her mother's objections thwarted a suitor.

Walter, the second of five children, was born two years after his older brother Theodore. He was followed by Roy and Victor, his compatriots in the labor movement, and much later by a sister, Christine. As the children grew, Val Reuther's interest in working-class organizations, politics, and ideology deepened. Many evenings were spent in reading socialist political and economic works. Joining the Socialist party of America, then near the peak of its membership and influence, he campaigned for its presidential candidate, Eugene V. Debs; ran as a socialist for a seat in the state legislature; often spoke publicly in behalf of candidates and causes; and testified before legislative committees on matters of concern to workers. For Val Reuther, the heart of socialism was its promise of equal opportunity for all and freedom from arbitrary power and human exploitation. His goal was a just society gained democratically through persuasion and votes, not the proletarian dictatorship of revolutionary Marxism.

The Reuther family knew the struggles, deprivations, and insecurities of the working class. Flour and sugar sacks were turned into sheets and underwear, and when Walter mischievously used an umbrella as a parachute, its fabric was salvaged for a hand-sewn waterproof shirt. The boys found part-time jobs. Walter delivered newspapers and worked in a glass factory and a bakery.

With the rise of the prohibition movement, which threatened all brewery workers, West Virginia brewery owners and workers cooperated in an effort to stem the tide. Val Reuther, on leave from his job, traveled throughout the state for three months speaking against a proposed prohibitionist constitutional amendment. Nevertheless, in 1912 the voters approved the amendment, to take effect in two years. When Val consequently lost his job, the family survived by taking in roomers, operating a small cafe, and even bootlegging beer across the river from Ohio. Their income was small and uncertain, however, until several years later, when Val became an agent for a life insurance company and, with fellow workers for clients, attained modest prosperity and security.

Within the family, Walter mastered the vocabulary of labor and reform and the techniques of effective speaking and debate. When the Lutheran pastor attacked unions from the pulpit, Val Reuther denounced him before the congregation and withdrew from the church; but Anna insisted that she and the boys continue to attend. After Sunday services, Val questioned them closely and critically on the day's sermon. From this dialogue emerged a tradition of Sunday afternoon debates, with the four boys divided into two sides and locked in intense verbal combat, with Val Reuther as timekeeper, referee, and judge. In preparation the boys studied current controversial topics at home and in the public library—regulation and abolition of child labor, woman suffrage, government regulation of business, public ownership of railroads. The Reuthers occasionally discussed subjects as abstruse as class conflict and socialism, but usually their debates were drawn directly from current public issues of interest to workers. Walter, like the others, became a powerful, self-assured speaker, with inexhaustible verbal energy and an effortless capacity to weave ideas and facts into a persuasive message.

Val Reuther introduced his sons to the gospel of trade unions and social democracy, and he taught them to revere the martyrs of that faith. In 1919 he took the eleven-year-old Walter and his younger brother Victor to call on Eugene V. Debs, then incarcerated in the Moundsville, West Virginia, federal prison, sentenced to ten years for criticizing wartime government policies. Debs greeted his friend and the boys with his customary warmth and affection. After they left, Val Reuther wept for the only time in Victor's recollection, murmuring in despair, "How can they imprison so kind and gentle a man?"

Like many unskilled workers, Val Reuther urged his sons to prepare for a skilled trade or to gain the education necessary to enter a profession. At sixteen, before graduation, Walter left high school to work for the Wheeling Steel Company as an apprentice die maker, starting at only 11 cents an hour. For several years he had excelled in shop classes, liking metalworking so much that he had largely given up sports and other activites in order to spend time after school in the machine shop. Die makers were the elite of the metalworking trades, producing precision hardened steel forms for use in presses and other metal-shaping machines. When he left after three years, his rate had advanced to 42 cents. Although he never completed the apprenticeship, he nonetheless mastered the skills of the demanding die maker's craft. A quick and eager worker, and already a crusader for a better deal for workers, he was attracted to Detroit, whose automobile factories made it America's metalworking center.

In 1927 exciting changes in car manufacturing drew many workers to the Motor City. The Ford Motor Company, belatedly preparing to replace the Model T with a new car, would soon embark on the largest rebuilding and renewal of an industrial property in history. Skilled mechanics were leaving Wheeling and other cities for auto jobs in Detroit. In February 1927 Reuther drove to Detroit with a friend in hopes of better pay, more challenging work, and a chance to complete high school.

Although the future looked bright, jobs were hard to find when Reuther arrived. Ford, the area's largest employer, had laid off thousands of workers as it wound down production of the Model T. Reuther tramped the streets and stood in employment lines before landing a job as a drill press operator on the night shift at Briggs Manufacturing Company, a major supplier of bodies to Ford. In order to win contracts, independent firms had to produce car parts for less than it cost the auto companies themselves to make them. Their wage rates were often low, and they drove the workers hard. By reputation Briggs was the industry's worst employer; the long hours and rapid pace of its machines left employees exhausted, and accidents were so common in the pressed steel department that it was known as "the butcher shop." When streetcar conductors called out "the slaughterhouse!" Briggs workers knew the car had reached their stop. Reuther earned 60 cents an hour, well above his Wheeling pay, and worked a ten- to twelve-hour night shift.

Eager to work at the die maker's trade, Reuther remained at Briggs only a few weeks. He soon sought employment with Ford, which was beginning to hire for production of its new Model A. The company advertised for die leaders—those with years of experience who could direct twenty or more workers in building complicated dies for presses from blueprints. Reuther, though only nineteen and scarcely qualified for the job, nevertheless applied. The company's master mechanic resented this brash youngster's waste of his time; but when Reuther demanded and passed a blueprint test, the mechanic, impressed but not yet convinced, proposed an experiment. Reuther would work for two days without knowing his pay, and then the company would decide whether to keep him. Walter agreed and hurried to Briggs for his machinists' tools, but his supervisor there tried to persuade him to stay by offering a raise and refusing to allow Reuther to remove his tools from the plant. He was unable to leave until the end of the night shift, when he rushed back to Ford to put in a full day under the skeptical eyes of the master mechanic and a foreman. Although he had not slept in two days, he was hired, not as die leader but as a die maker at $1.05 an hour, more than twice his Wheeling wage only a few weeks before. Self-confidence, persistence, and sheer stamina had paid off.

Reuther worked at Ford for five years. Until the depression, both wages and responsibilities rose steadily. His highest rate of pay, late in 1929 when he was classified as an "A-1 Diemaker Leader" (a foreman's position) was $1.40 an hour. Although hard times drove his wages down to $1.00 an hour by 1932, this was still enough to place him among the wage-earning elite. Production workers lucky enough to have a job were making only $4.00 a day.

Away from work, Reuther completed high school, enrolling at Fordson High in Dearborn for a full schedule of classes in the

morning, followed by a factory shift until midnight. Homework
filled the remaining hours. An English class essay recounted the
furious pace of a typical day:

> The race is on. First a few hurried calisthenics; the dash to the
> bathroom, before someone else beats me there. . . . I finish break-
> fast, dash back to my room; the clock says, "Four minutes till your
> Geometry class starts." I grab my hat and books, and start down
> Horger Avenue on a run. Down the hall, to my locker, and to my
> Geometry class. Hot and out of breath, I enter the room as the bell
> rings to end the first lap.

While in school, Reuther presided over the 4C Club ("cooperation, confidence, comradeship, and citizenship") formed
by working students. On the application for membership he
wrote: "I realize that to do something constructive in life, one
must have an education. I seek knowledge that I may serve
mankind."

In 1930 Victor Reuther joined Walter in Detroit, where they
lived in a cooperative house with three friends who worked at
Ford. With millions of workers unemployed, the depression
bolstered the brothers' belief in socialism's message of jobs and
security through national economic planning and coordination.
In the morning the young men attended classes at Detroit City
College (later Wayne State University), and the four Ford workers went to their jobs in the afternoon. Vic, unable to find work,
managed the cooperative. In spare moments he traveled about
the city observing the social wreckage left in the depression's
wake. On weekends he guided the others on tours of the city's
Hoovervilles, the shantytowns of cardboard and corrugated tin
that housed the unemployed. To share the experiences of the
down and out, they spent a night in a Salvation Army flophouse,
where they were fed and deloused before going to bed.

Study and action went hand in hand. At Detroit City College,
as all over the country, professors and students sought the
answers to the perplexing questions of the times: Why had the
economic system failed? What should be done? Walter and Vic

joined the Socialist party and frequented its Detroit headquarters, where they met like-minded young people and prominent socialists such as Norman Thomas. At the college they organized a Social Problems Club dedicated to social study and action. Affiliated with the League for Industrial Democracy, a socialist youth organization, the club sposored debates and forums, brought in speakers, distributed literature, and prosecuted its causes—successfully opposing the establishment of a campus ROTC unit, for example, and desegregating a college swimming pool. When the Detroit Board of Education fired a professor opposed to the ROTC, the protests of Walter and Vic won his reinstatement. The brothers prepared a pamphlet on rich and poor in Detroit, with a text excoriating capitalism and photographs contrasting the suburban homes of the wealthy with the shacks and hovels of the city's unemployed, the "homes that a dying social order is providing for its . . . workers."

In the midst of despair, the 1932 presidential contest stirred the hopes of socialists. Herbert Hoover and Franklin D. Roosevelt, the candidates of the major parties, conceded little to the need for economic and social reconstruction. For the first time since 1920, the Socialist party, with Norman Thomas as its candidate, mounted a spirited campaign.

Eager to take part, Reuther installed a small speaker's platform in place of the rumble seat of his Model A Ford, and toured southeastern Michigan giving speeches wherever he could gather an audience. One day in Dearborn, which was virtually a company town of the Ford Motor Company, he drove the car onto a lot, mounted the platform, and launched into a speech for Thomas. The police tried to end the meeting, charging Reuther with speaking on private property without permission. When he produced the deed to the lot, the officers retreated but would not admit defeat; they staked out the lot's boundaries and warned his many listeners not to trespass on neighboring properties.

Reuther organized Thomas for President clubs on college campuses in Michigan, Ohio, and Indiana, and served as chairman of the midwestern district of the National Student

Committee for Thomas. He noted in a letter to the committee's director that the socialist cause "to me has become as dear as life itself." At the end of October he reported that more than half of the colleges in his district had Thomas for President clubs, including one at Detroit City College with a membership of nearly two hundred.

Val Reuther, proud and gratified that his sons had embraced a cause so dear to him, wrote them: "To me Socialism is the star of hope that lights the way, leading the workers from wage slavery to social justice, and to know that you boys have joined the movement, and are doing all in your power to spread a doctrine of equal opportunities for all mankind, only tends to increase my love." With every word they spoke in behalf of justice, Walter and Vic fulfilled their father's hope. He had defined what would remain the goal of their activity even after Walter ceased to be a socialist in name: equal opportunities for all mankind.

During the campaign Reuther was laid off at Ford's. Perhaps the company's decision was strictly economic, but Reuther suspected that his political activities or his membership in the tiny but militant left-wing Auto Workers Union was involved. In any case, Walter and Victor had talked for months of an educational trip to Europe to gain firsthand exposure to the upheavals that were occurring there. Now that neither had work, they were free to go. Walter, always frugal, had saved enough money to finance a tour of Germany, France, and England. Their ultimate destination was the Soviet Union, where they hoped for a longer stay, to be supported by jobs at the Molotov Auto Works in Gorki. The Soviet government had purchased Ford's production machinery for the Model A, and die makers were needed to maintain the machines and teach the trade to unskilled Russians. Several Ford workers had already gone to the Gorki plant, including a communist friend of Reuther's, who encouraged him to apply. Walter would be a valuable employee. The Soviets agreed to employ Victor also, although he had no training as a machinist. During a vacation in Wheeling, Walter put Victor through a crash course at the high school shop. At a farewell party Walter assured the gathering that they were going to "study the economic and social conditions of the world, not the bright lights." With these lofty intentions they sailed from New York for Germany on February 15, 1933. They would not return to the United States for nearly three years.

* * *

In early 1933 Germany was in crisis, as Hitler and the Nazis forced their way to power. Although the brothers had known of conditions there in a general way, they were shocked by the violence, oppression, and civic disintegration they encountered. They arrived only a few days before the burning of the Reichstag building in Berlin, the seat of the legislature. Its destruction was exploited by the Nazis, who accused the Communists of plotting a seizure of power. Walter and Victor were conducted through the smoldering ruins by a Nazi guide.

Letters of introduction from Norman Thomas led them to socialist students and workers, and they attended somber political meetings before the election of March 1933. Since the forces opposed to Hitler would not unite and the Nazis would do anything to win, the socialists prepared for the worst. In the student cooperative where they lived, windows and doors were barred, a round-the-clock watch was set up, and a rope ladder was placed near a back window to allow residents to evade capture. The Nazis' victory in the election, in which they won a parliamentary majority and control of the government with 44 percent of the vote, encouraged their paramilitary units to attack and crush their socialist and communist enemies as quickly and ruthlessly as possible. At 3:00 A.M. of the morning following the election, the socialists' house was raided by Nazi toughs in pursuit of a young socialist trade unionist whom the Reuthers helped to escape. The storm troopers made some arrests and, after examining the Reuthers' passports, advised them to find new lodgings and new companions. The next day the storm troopers and police raided trade union and Social Democratic party headquarters.

When the Reuthers left Berlin "almost stunned by events," they discovered that nazism had divided all Germans. In their mother's village of Scharnhausen, one uncle, a printer, was a union member and a Social Democrat. Another uncle—a farmer, deputy mayor of his village, and a Nazi—presented his nephews with a photograph of himself mounted on a farm horse, wearing the swastika arm band and giving the Nazi salute. Everywhere they saw the Nazi tide spreading. Independent organizations of workers were stamped out. In Scharnhausen, the Workers' Singing Society had to change its name and was then forbidden to meet. Every house had to fly the Nazi party's swastika flag on the German memorial day. At a large demonstration, Hitler Youth led the crowd in shouting, "Heil Hitler." When a Communist flag was thrown on a bonfire, an onlooker who shouted, "You stole that," was beaten. The townspeople were embarrassed that the assault was witnessed by the two Americans.

With relief the Reuthers left Germany for a bicycle tour of less troubled nations. They rode through the Black Forest, down the Rhone Valley of France, and along the Riviera into Italy, stopping at youth hostels or sleeping in fields. In Rome, however, fascist spectacles were a bitter reminder of Germany as Mussolini, the Italian dictator, worked the crowds into hysteria. Returning north to Vienna, the brothers were favorably impressed by the progressive achievements of the Austrian socialists and trade unionists in providing housing, medical care, libraries, and day care centers. Further travels took them to England and the Netherlands.

On their return to Germany, the Reuthers entered a dark and dangerous world by becoming couriers in an underground communications network established by socialists and trade unionists to carry on resistance to Hitler. The messages had to be memorized to avoid carrying incriminating papers. On one mission the brothers' contact was Fritz in Gelsenkirchen in the Ruhr. They had no address but were simply directed to a bookshop in Dortmund, where they were to ask for a certain rare book. Shunted through a labyrinth of shops to avoid detection, they finally reached Fritz and delivered their messages.

Almost out of money and fearful of remaining in Germany, the brothers were desperate to depart for the Soviet Union but still lacked visas. Perhaps as a consequence of United States diplomatic recognition of the USSR, Soviet approval came through, clearing their way to Gorki. They left Berlin by train for Moscow on November 15, 1933.

Two days later they arrived in the Soviet capital in knickers, thin stockings, and light jackets with the temperature 35 degrees below zero. Footlockers containing their heavy clothing had been sent ahead to Gorki, where it was just as cold. The only Russian word they knew was *avtozavod*—"auto factory." With that, they found the correct streetcar for the six-mile ride to the plant. After they arrived, they discovered that their jackets had been slit and papers and some money stolen. Thanks to money belts, however, their passports and hard currency were safe.

They lived in the Commune Ruthenberg, named for an American Communist but usually known as the American Village. It consisted of a dozen plain two-story apartment buildings, some communal rooms, and a store where only foreigners could shop. They were given a room so small that they had to hang their bicycles and footlockers from the ceiling to conserve space.

The Russians were still building the massive Gorki plant, one of the major undertakings of the First Five-Year Plan, when the Reuthers arrived. In 1929 the Ford Motor Company signed a complex agreement with the Soviets calling for the training of technicians, the dispatch of Ford experts to the USSR, and the sale of the Model A dies and other machinery. Four years later, however, few Soviet cars had yet been made. The unheated die and tool room, with its temperature below zero, was housed in a vast building used mostly for making wheels and brake drums. Fortunately, its location next to the heat-treat department, where die metals were hardened in high-temperature furnaces, allowed the Reuthers (wearing sheepskin coats beneath their shop aprons) to work at their benches for a half hour before rushing into heat-treat to thaw out their nearly frozen fingers.

Although many foreigners worked in the plant, the force of 32,000 was predominantly Soviet citizens, few with technical skills. Either former peasants or seminomadic tribesmen from central Asia, scarcely any had industrial or urban experience. One family, accustomed to living in tents, built a fire on the wooden floor of their flat to prepare meals. Their baggy peasant blouses and trousers were hazardous amid the factory's whirling shafts and gears. Victor later reported in a letter to the *Moscow Daily News*, an English language newspaper published for foreign workers, that a shop committee had persuaded the authorities to purchase aprons for those in the tool and die room.

Production improved gradually as the foreign tradesmen and Soviet workers made necessary adjustments and learned from each other. Since almost no one understood English, the Reuthers at first gave instruction in German, which was then translated into Russian. Soon, however, they absorbed enough of the native language for their purposes. As Russians learned the trades, they took on more responsibility. When the Reuthers arrived, the toolroom work force of 800, including 172 women, produced only one complete die every three weeks. When they left eighteen months later, it produced five or six each month. The work week of forty-eight hours was slightly shorter than that in predepression United States auto plants.

Reuther keenly felt the obstacles the USSR faced, and he tried to eliminate inefficiency and increase production. In an interview with a Moscow newspaper, he argued that the progress of the Soviet workers had far outstripped the ability of the administrative apparatus to manage the process. The workers, he thought, were "amazing"; but management, bogged down in "reams of red tape" and cramped by overcentralization of authority, lagged behind.

Praise and affection for the Soviet workers accompanied Reuther's sharp criticism of Soviet factory management. The workers' morale in the Gorki plant—the "human aspects"—far exceeded that in the Citroën, Mercedes-Benz, and other European auto factories he had visited, let alone that in United States factories. "To a Ford worker especially," Reuther wrote, the social and cultural life of the Russian factory was "absorbing." He expanded on this theme: "In the Red Corner at lunch intervals a wonderful spirit of camaraderie is found among the workers. A foreman produces a guitar, strums a few chords, a greasy mechanic and a red-kerchiefed Komsomolka, forgetting work, swing into gay dancing. Everybody keeps rhythm, shouts and laughs. I enjoy every moment here!" The determination of a backward people to create a better life through an immense cooperative effort excited Reuther's admiration.

Although the Reuthers remained enthusiastic about Soviet industrial progress—as letters of glowing praise to friends testified—the tyranny of the regime intruded ominously before many months had passed. An Italian worker living at Gorki with his family was arrested in a midnight police raid. The next day a story circulated that, as a follower of Stalin's banished rival Leon Trotsky, the Italian had been exiled to Siberia. There was no trial, and he was neither seen nor heard from again. The assassination of Kirov, the Communist party leader in Leningrad, in December 1934, marked a new phase in the purge of Stalin's enemies. Victor claimed that he and Walter were not misled by the official charge of Trotsky's responsibility. "After our experiences in Germany, Walter and I were not deceived when Stalin, Molotov, Beria, Khrushchev, and others hurried to Leningrad with expressions of shock, sadness and concern to attribute the killing to a Trotskyist plot."

Kirov was shot by a party member named Nikolayev. Portions of his trial were broadcast over the Gorki plant's public address system during lunch breaks, with meetings organized to "review the evidence" that linked Nikolayev to Trotsky and to adopt resolutions calling for condemnation and revenge. The purge spread. Anyone could come under suspicion, and arrests by the secret police became common. Open political discussion ceased. "It was only on those rare occasions when we were alone with friends on a walk through the woods or perhaps in a rowboat in the middle of the Oka," Victor continued, "that we could talk to any Russian worker about his opinion of the Stalin regime and the political oppression that was hanging like a sword over his head."

As their time in the USSR drew to a close, the Reuthers had mixed feelings. They admired and respected the monumental undertakings and accomplishments of Soviet industrialization. They were confident that most Russians were working at better jobs, eating better food, receiving better education, and obtaining better medical care than they had known before. Women played an active, varied role; children seemed well cared for and happy. On the other hand, mounting evidence of a sinister, brutal authoritarianism cast a chilling shadow over all that had been achieved.

The Reuthers intended only a sojourn in the USSR, not permanent residence. In 1935 they returned to the United States, continuing across the Soviet Union and the Pacific Ocean so that their trip took them around the world. With the relatively good pay in Gorki and the little on which to spend it there, they had accumulated a comfortable sum in nonconvertible rubles to expend on travel in the USSR. Furthermore, as *udarniks*— workers who had exceeded production quotas—they qualified for travel privileges.

They first swung through southern Russia and the Ukraine, visiting public works projects like the giant dam under construction on the Dneiper River, collective farms, and Black Sea resorts in the Crimea. They hiked up through the Caucasus Mountains; crossed the Caspian Sea by steamer to Samarkand; and then went to Tashkent, seeing areas that few foreign travelers were then allowed to glimpse. Eventually they returned to Moscow to board a Trans-Siberian train for the long trip to Manchuria and China, where scenes of suffering and injustice disturbed them. The worst of several incidents they witnessed occurred as they boarded a river boat in Nanking. A crowd of destitute peasants gathered at the dock to force their way onto the departing boat. The owners had hired a band of Sikhs armed with clubs to block the way. Victor recalled: "As the peasants fought to get on board, grabbing the railings, they were savagely clubbed, and sank in the muddy waters beneath us. No one made any effort to save them from drowning, and when we protested, we were told that they would soon have died of starvation anyway! I have never before or since felt as horrified—and as helpless."

From China the Reuthers went to Japan for a brief tour and found much to delight them. Running low on funds, they worked their way across the Pacific on an American liner, Walter as a wiper in the engine room and Victor as a deckhand. When they landed in Los Angeles, they had been away nearly three years.

Politically, Reuther was a left-wing democratic socialist. At that time the entire left, communist and socialist, was being urged to unite in a Popular Front against the reactionary menace of nazism and fascism. Although communists and democratic socialists were divided over revolutionary, as opposed to evolutionary, methods of change and other matters of doctrine and tactics, events in Germany had demonstrated that the left's only chance of success—even of survival—lay in cooperation. The possibility of war created still stronger pressures for a united left. In 1934 a war scare in the USSR, provoked by hostile statements from Hitler and German rearmament, brought Red Army engineers into the Gorki plant to supervise the building of dies for military truck and tank parts. Soon the outbreak of civil war in Spain would match left against right on the battlefield. Beleaguered by powerful enemies, the customarily quarrelsome left sought to save itself through alliance. Although differences over authoritarian versus democratic methods and the exploitation of foreign communists to advance Soviet national interests would eventually divide the left again, for a time the need for a Popular Front alliance was dictated both by fear of a powerful enemy and by a hope that a united left could accomplish constructive changes.

In the United States the Roosevelt administration, from which the left had originally expected little, was encouraging workers to establish and join unions. Workers in previously untouched industries, like auto manufacturing, were organizing. When the Reuthers returned in the fall of 1935, American organized labor stood on the verge of its greatest expansion, sparked by a new spirit of militance and determination. The brothers were eager to take part in the coming struggle.

II

Auto Workers Before the Union

THE UNITED STATES AUTOMOBILE INDUSTRY in 1935 was a stricken giant. Its 1929 production of 5.5 million vehicles had made it the largest manufacturing operation in the world. In 1932 production bottomed out at 1.3 million, recovering to 4 million in 1935, only to drop sharply again in late 1937. Full production and employment returned only with a new decade and the approach of war.

Expanding markets, rapid growth, and great rewards as well as risks marked the auto industry's early years, prompting hundreds of firms to try their hand at car manufacturing. Most of these were assemblers that bought parts on credit from suppliers and put them together. With small capital requirements and a buoyant market, the business was competitive and uncertain. Companies folded as rapidly as new ones appeared, or were absorbed by larger firms, with the result that the giants—first Ford, then General Motors, and later Chrysler— gradually emerged. By the end of the 1920s, although several important independents—including Packard, Hudson, Studebaker, and Willys—remained, the industry had become an oligopoly, with its production dominated by three massive firms.

The auto industry also consolidated geographically to attain greater efficiency and reduce transportation costs. Manufacturing, once carried on in many states, eventually centered in Detroit and the southern Michigan cities of Flint, Lansing, and Pontiac. A secondary ring of assembly and parts plants ran through Ohio, Indiana, Wisconsin, and southwestern Ontario, with an occasional outpost in other regions.

The composition of the labor force changed gradually as well. At first most workers were skilled—three-quarters of those in Michigan automobile plants as late as 1910. Machinists, molders, foundrymen, upholsterers, cabinetmakers, and others in the metal and woodworking trades supplied labor for the early cars. Mounting demand, however, produced a severe labor shortage that drove up the wages commanded by skilled workers. Labor-saving machinery, the obvious solution to rising costs, could be manned by cheaper unskilled or semiskilled workers.

Accessible by water, rail, and road transport, Detroit had an excellent location for attracting the masses of unskilled workers that mechanization and high-volume production required. Throughout the Great Lakes region men and families migrated to the city from farms, country towns, abandoned lumber camps, and mines. Thousands of immigrant Poles, Italians, Hungarians, and southern Slavs came also. Few of these migrants, foreigners and country boys alike, had industrial experience. Accustomed to poverty, divided by language, religion, and habits; lacking craft skills; and usually suspicious of unions, they provided the bulk of the industry's quickly trained, semiskilled work force but seemed unpromising recruits for organized labor.

The city that received these newcomers, like most other turn-of-the-century cities, had numerous strong craft unions of skilled workers—as many as eighty-seven in Detroit in 1904. At first it appeared that the advent of a growing, relatively high-wage industry would augment union power; but several forces— such as the use of machines and assembly lines manned by unskilled labor, ethnic fragmentation of the work force, insecurity of employment due to seasonal production, and the implacable opposition of the leading car manufacturers— undermined that expectation, turning Detroit in a few years into the nation's leading open shop city, where no worker could be forced to join a union and collective bargaining was rare. The Employers' Association led the city's business leaders in an attack on unions through propaganda, blacklists, and the use of scabs. By the end of the decade, the association could truthfully assert that "the open shop exists in Detroit as it exists nowhere else."

The most significant and celebrated experiments in production methods and industrial relations took place at the Ford Motor Company. In 1913 the company introduced the continuously moving assembly line at its Highland Park factory. As Henry Ford's ghostwriter later analyzed the process, it consisted of "focussing upon a manufacturing project . . . the principles of power, accuracy, economy, system, continuity, speed, and repetition." Although individual elements and concepts of the assembly line—such as interchangeable parts, conveyors, coordination, and flow process—had been used before, the Ford organization created from them a new system that could be rationalized and extended indefinitely. In a few months the company reduced the labor time required for assembling a Model T chassis from 12.5 to only 1.5 man-hours; it then cut prices, inducing a soaring demand for the product. As the Model Ts poured from Ford factories, the assembly line was hailed as the miracle of modern manufacturing.

Mechanization and the assembly line transformed the typical auto worker into a machine tender whose job could be learned in days or even hours. By the 1920s auto-manufacturing processes were more thoroughly subdivided and standardized than those of any other large industry. Henry Ford claimed that 43 percent of the manual jobs in his factories required only a day's training, and an additional 36 percent no more than a week. As reported in 1924, 40 percent of the workers in a typical auto plant were machine tenders, with another 45 percent equally divided among assemblers, helpers, and laborers, making a total of 85 percent in unskilled or semiskilled classifications. Only 10 percent were skilled tradesmen, and 5 percent were inspectors or testers. These proportions would change little in future years.

The shift to a semiskilled and unskilled work force opened up new sources of labor. White southerners from Tennessee, Kentucky, Arkansas, Alabama, and Mississippi headed north for the auto cities during World War I, when jobs were certain and pay good. By the 1920s sections of Detroit, Pontiac, and Flint had a strong southern flavor. In some factories, more than half of new hires were southerners, often part of a transient "suitcase brigade," arriving by bus or train in the spring when the plants were hiring and then moving on or returning south when layoffs hit the industry. Individualistic, lacking industrial and urban experience, these transient workers looked like a good hedge against unions to the Employers Association of Detroit.

With southern whites came southern blacks. The black population of Detroit increased sixfold between 1910 and 1920. Many came in response to recruiting campaigns mounted by employment agencies, bus companies, and in a few instances the auto manufacturers themselves. The Ford Motor Company was known for employing blacks, and this reputation was a major lure. Although conditions in the plants and crowded cities left a lot to be desired, they were often an improvement over the shanties and depleted lands of the rural South. Joe Louis, the future Brown Bomber, recalled:

> I was twelve years old when Pat Brooks heard about the money Ford was paying. He went up first, then brought us up to Detroit. We moved in with some of our kin in MacComb Street. It was kind of crowded there, but the house had toilets indoors and electric lights. Down in Alabama we had outhouses and kerosene lamps. My stepfather got a job with Ford, and we got a place of our own in a frame tenement in Catherine Street.

In 1926, out of 100,000 local employees of Ford, about 10,000 were blacks. Other Detroit companies—such as Hupp with 12 percent, Studebaker with 10 percent, and Cadillac with 5 percent—had some black employees, but many firms had none. One survey found 30,000 black wage earners in Detroit, about half of them employed in manufacturing and foundry work in the auto industry.

Nearly all the blacks were employed in unskilled manual work. Usually, as one Ford official put it, they "do work that nobody else would do." At Ford they could be found in the foundry, at rough, dirty, noisy, and dangerous jobs, and as laborers and maintenance men, although some blacks did work on assembly lines. At Chrysler they were used almost exclusively in disagreeable and unhealthful paint shops.

Although massive immigration of foreigners ended in 1914 with the outbreak of World War I, foreign-born workers and their descendants—Poles, Russians, Italians, Hungarians, Austrians, and Belgians—predominated in many of the large Detroit plants for years. Dodge, for example, reported in 1928 that fifty-seven nationalities were represented in its work force. Of nearly 100,000 Detroit auto workers listed in the 1930 census as "operatives" or "laborers," 42 percent were foreign born. Smaller but significant numbers of Canadian and British migrants were present, especially in the skilled trades, along with second-generation representatives of the earlier immigrants, particularly Germans. Like Reuther, they tended to look with more favor on unions and radical politics than did most auto workers.

As with blacks, the number of female employees in Michigan's automobile and allied factories increased during the 1920s, to over 5 percent of the work force. Women worked as assemblers; as press, crane, and hoist operators; as welders, polishers, sanders, and grinders—in all kinds of jobs except the very heaviest. They tended to be concentrated in those jobs requiring hand or other close work, such as finishing, polishing, upholstery, and inspection.

Trimming costs was always a leading management objective, and the employment of women was an effective cost-cutting device. A Michigan law outlawing discrimination "in any way in the payment of wages as between sex" was seldom enforced. A 1925 study found that the average earnings of women in the industry were 47 cents an hour, compared with 73 cents for men. A Ford worker laid off in 1927 reported that his wife landed a job running a drill press for 30 cents an hour, half of what he had received for the same work: "She could do the work as well as I could so the firm hired her because she was cheaper. If she had refused some other woman would have taken it." Michigan law restricted women to ten hours of work a day and fifty-four a week. Some companies were said to order women to punch the time card when they reached the maximum and then return to their jobs for another hour or two.

Costs could also be reduced by hiring the young, who—since increasingly the work required strength, stamina, and energy rather than skill—were well qualified. Older employees receiving full pay were replaced by beginners on probationary rates. Employers made no secret of their preference for young workers; some companies simply refused to hire anyone beyond a certain age. At Ford's Highland Park factory, three-quarters of the employees were under forty. Periods of slack production were convenient occasions for lowering the average age of the work force. In 1928, following a model changeover, Hudson hired thousands of new workers of both sexes, all young and all lower paid than those they replaced. Hair dye sold well in Detroit drug stores.

Competition stimulated other cost-cutting experiments. Parts makers were usually paid on a piecework basis, but line production could not easily be broken down into units of work. The line could be speeded up at the touch of a button, however, forcing workers to step up their pace or risk creating a jam. "Holding up the line" was the cardinal sin. In 1925 Ford plants produced 31,200 cars a week with the same machinery and work force that had made only 25,000 a week in 1920. Workers were sometimes pushed beyond endurance. As one auto worker complained during the depression to President Franklin D. Roosevelt, the moving assembly line "means that human flesh and blood with souls and ideals is placed in competition with and paced by a mechanical robot which never tires. . . . If Simon

Legree were to come back to life and see a modern conveyor line in operation, when it is really strutting its stuff, he would dig Uncle Tom up and kick Hell out of him because of not doing anywhere near his possibilities."

Hours of work averaged about fifty per week during the 1920s, not excessive by the standards of the times. The usual pattern was nine hours a day for five and a half days. Hours varied seasonally as slack time and layoff alternated with hectic activity and overtime. A 1925 study showed that fewer than half the plants surveyed paid a higher rate for overtime. Some workers put in overtime for no additional pay as a condition of holding a job.

Hourly rates of pay went up as a consequence of mass production and booming sales. In the most startling event in the history of wages, Ford declared in January 1914 that he would pay $5.00 a day, more than $2.00 above prevailing rates, an increase of fully 75 percent. The company said its decision merely gave the worker his due: with consumers, stockholders, and management all benefiting from the Model T's success, it only remained to acknowledge the worker's contribution. A desire to share the company's wealth figured in the decision, but there were other considerations as well. By paying high wages, Ford could get the pick of the labor force, diminish the problem of turnover, and quiet the stirrings of unrest among workers.

Ford's announcement left the country thunderstruck. With the exception of Ford's competitors, there was universal acclaim. Applicants besieged the employment office, with ten thousand at a time gathering at the gates. Panicked officials, fearing a riot, once dispersed the mass of job seekers with streams of water from high-pressure hoses in a temperature of 9 degrees above zero.

The new rate was not granted across the board, however. Ford required a minimum age of twenty-one, as well as a six-month residence in Detroit followed by a six-month probationary period in the plant. Female employees and office workers were excluded at first, but within two years the rate was extended to them. By 1916 three-quarters of Ford's employees were on the new wage scale.

At the same time, Ford launched an experiment in employer paternalism designed to use economic incentives to shape the character and habits of his employees. The controversial, ambitious program served to undermine employees' gratitude for higher wages. Many businessmen, including Ford, feared that increased wages would only be wasted. Money might be thrown away on drink or amusements, or hoarded by immigrant workers planning to return to their homelands. Thus the Ford Company established a sociological department, with 150 investigators, to determine whether higher wages would be well used. They visited workers in their homes to obtain answers to a long list of questions, including marital status, nationality, religion, prospects for citizenship if an alien, home ownership, health, recreations, and the total of debts and savings. The investigators were instructed to observe habits and home and neighborhood conditions. Employees could be excluded for bad personal habits, such as an excessive use of liquor, gambling, or "any malicious practise derogatory to good physical manhood or moral character." A disqualified worker was placed on probation. If he reformed within thirty days, all the sums withheld were paid; if reform required sixty days, he got only three-quarters; and so on in descending amounts. Finally, after six months, if still intractable, he was fired. A worker who did not know English was required to attend language classes. Within a few years Ford lost interest in such paternalistic reform of morals and behavior. Since many workers had resented such close scrutiny of their lives, however, it left a residue of suspicion.

Ford's reputation for good pay persisted, but the entire picture was less rosy. Other manufacturers eventually raised their wages close to Ford's level. In 1928, the last outstandingly prosperous year, auto workers earned 75 cents an hour, compared with 56 cents for all manufacturing workers. The seasonal character of auto employment qualified these high rates, however, since companies laid off workers in slack times. During the 1920s the annual real wages of auto workers were only a little higher than those of all manual workers. In addition to irregular earnings, wage grievances included the use of piece rates in parts manufacturing and of complicated bonus payments instead of straight time.

Even more serious than inadequate or irregular wages was the victimization of workers by the arbitrary exercise of power. Foremen were the focus of insecurity and outrage. Originally they hired and fired in their departments with little restraint, and the unscrupulous exploited their power on and even off the job. A foreman might order a worker to paint his house, wash his car, cut his grass, or do other household chores on the worker's "day off" or after work in order to keep his job. Management in many companies recognized that favoritism, exploitation, and bribery were problems but hesitated to restrict the authority of those immediately responsible for production and discipline. The Ford Motor Company reduced the role of its foremen in 1914 by establishing an employment office. In most companies, however, even where seniority was nominally recognized for layoff and rehire, the foreman continued to be the key determinant of equity in the workplace. Beneath the surface calm of labor relations before the Great Depression flowed massive under-currents of unrest and dissatisfaction. The explosive outbursts of militancy in the 1930s, sparked by the depression, drew on years of suppressed resentment.

If the workers had grievances, unions could provide a way of dealing with them. Prior to the depression, however, all efforts to establish an auto workers' union had failed. Detroit seemed to deserve its reputation as the "graveyard of organizers." An American Federation of Labor (AFL) affiliate, the Carriage, Wagon and Automobile Workers' International, showed interest but encountered opposition both from the companies and from rival craft unions. In 1918, after suspension from the AFL, it set out to organize the workers on the principle of industrial unionism—that is, a union including all the workers in a plant regardless of the particular job or skill of each. A few joined, but the recession of 1920 reduced the union to a paper organization.

On two occasions during the 1920s the AFL made feeble efforts to unionize auto workers. Its attempt to apply the craft principle of organization to a mass of unskilled workers guaranteed failure, however. In 1920 its executive council instructed each of the eight trade unions with claims to a portion of the auto workers to assign an organizer, but nothing happened. The 1926 AFL convention approved a plan calling for the assignment of craft workers to the appropriate affiliated trade union and the recruitment of the remainder into organizations called federal labor unions, which were linked directly to the AFL. Later, if all went according to plan, the members of the federal labor unions would be parceled out among the affiliated trade unions. A few organizers went to Detroit, where they encountered hostility from the manufacturers and indifference among the workers. The campaign director attempted to persuade Henry Ford "to try collective bargaining," but Ford was not interested.

Leftist labor organizations may have shown more vitality, but they produced no better result. The Industrial Workers of the World (IWW), the militant Wobblies of the prewar era, organized auto workers but disappeared following an unsuccessful strike at Studebaker in 1913. Communists also took an interest in auto workers; they launched an organizing drive in Detroit in 1925. Taking over a local of the nearly memberless auto and carriage workers' union, they renamed it the Auto Workers Union (AWU) and affiliated with the Trade Union Unity League, a communist labor federation. With small followings in a few Detroit factories, they published fugitive but militant shop papers and promoted the class struggle as well as they could.

* * *

The auto industry, a strapping and boisterous giant in its youth, proved vulnerable to the depression. Transformations in the marketplace and the shrinkage of consumer buying power ended its growth. By 1932, 80 percent of auto-building capacity, representing investments of hundreds of millions of dollars, lay idle. Employment had been cut in half and payrolls reduced by more than 60 percent. Average annual wages declined from $1,638 in 1929 to $1,035 in 1933, a drop of 37 percent for those lucky enough to hold a job. Although General Motors continued to show a profit, albeit much reduced, even strong firms suffered, and marginal companies went down by the score.

Detroit was harder hit than any other major United States metropolis. The average monthly case load of the city's welfare department increased from 5,000 in 1929 to nearly 50,000 in 1932. These figures understate the distress, since many families previously eligible for relief were removed from the rolls for lack of funds. A 1932 survey concluded that the city's population was caught in "a process of pauperizing, that is rapidly reducing the ... American citizen to ... insecurity and want, and destroying what had once been known as the American standard of living."

Conventional wisdom holds that depressions are not conducive to union activity. With jobs scarce and willing workers abundant, supply and demand do not favor those whose weapon is to withhold labor through a strike. Earlier depressions, however, had provoked spasms of united protest despite unfavorable economic odds. This one, the worst of all, proved no exception.

In the auto cities, with the strength of the open shop, the first organized responses to the depression were not strikes but demonstrations by the unemployed. Communists took the lead in setting up unemployed councils, about a dozen in and around Detroit. Although no more than two thousand party members lived there at the time, communist sympathizers and many other unemployed people, eager to strike any kind of blow, were ready to act. The councils organized demonstrations, demanded more welfare, and resisted evictions.

In March 1932 they chose Ford's River Rouge plant as the target of a protest march to demand jobs. The leaders were mainly communists, as were some of the marchers; but most of the three thousand persons gathered were simply unemployed workers, including many ex-Ford employees. "Nobody could look at the marchers themselves," the *Detroit News* wrote, "and accuse them of any destructive purpose." At the gates of the factory the Dearborn police, backed by the Ford Service Department, the plant security force, took their stand, drawing guns and firing into the crowd. Five marchers were killed and nineteen wounded. Rocks, bottles, and other missiles caused many casualties on both sides, among them Harry Bennett, the tough head of the Service Department. A funeral procession of ten thousand bore the martyrs to a common grave in the shadow of the Rouge's giant smokestacks. No other clash of those years more clearly revealed the anger unleashed by the depression.

By 1933, after four years of hard times, workers were ready to strike. Although the economy had not improved, the election of President Franklin D. Roosevelt and the launching of the New Deal stirred hope. Many employees and much of the public had lost confidence in the leadership and wisdom of businessmen. Troubles that once might have been borne as inevitable or as the price of a job became intolerable. A resurgent left, stimulated by the cries for change, struck responsive chords among the auto workers' rank and file with stormy denunciations of the economic system.

In 1933 "strikes just burst like lightning on the Detroit scene." The first serious one broke out at Briggs, which, with its low wages and hard driving of workers, remained a powder keg throughout the New Deal years. At the end of January, six thousand workers struck Briggs plants in Highland Park and Detroit, demanding higher wages and correction of harmful conditions. The inexperienced strikers had difficulty organizing themselves. The Auto Workers Union stepped in, prompting cries of "Red" domination by the newspapers and a refusal to bargain by the company. When the strike forced Ford, Briggs's most important customer, to shut down because of parts shortages, the company made limited concessions and resumed production at Highland Park. The largest of the Detroit plants, however, where fights on the picket lines between strikers and scabs continued for days, operated with only half of its pre-strike force for several weeks. Although Briggs made some concessions, the strikers failed to win most of their demands. About half of them lost their jobs, an unforgettable lesson in the risks involved. Nevertheless, the workers had shown their readiness to stand and fight. A current of revolt pulsed through the ranks.

In June 1933 Congress passed the National Industrial Recovery Act (NIRA), which set up complicated mechanisms to stimulate recovery. Section 7(a) of the law, a watershed in industrial relations, was the first federal guarantee of collective bargaining. It stated that employees had "the right to organize and bargain collectively through representatives of their own choosing" and that they must be free of "interference, restraint, or coercion" by employers in making this choice. The brave words rang hollow, however. Employers were not obligated in unambiguous language to recognize and bargain with representatives of the workers. The hastily drafted law failed to define "interference, restraint, or coercion," nor did it specify how workers' representatives were to be chosen. Thus company unions—those organized, financed, and favored by companies themselves—could enter the competition for workers' support. Regardless of the new law, workers still had to win a position in industry through their own efforts and strength.

Despite its imperfections, the NIRA's passage sparked an outburst of organizing activity. Unions that had been in decline launched ambitious campaigns, with John L. Lewis's United Mine Workers (UMW) and Sidney Hillman's Amalgamated Clothing Workers leading the charge. In the auto industry, where there was little base to build on, the government's benediction, bestowed through a vague, faulty law, brought rival organizations into the field.

From 1933 until 1936 the AFL, still wedded to craft unionism, conducted a flawed campaign to organize auto workers. President William Green sent an organizer, William Collins, to

Detroit to head the drive. His most serious handicap was the equivocal relationship of the AFL to the mass-production workers. Although Green recognized that unskilled production workers must be organized by industry since they had no trade, the chieftains of the craft international unions, indifferent or even hostile to industrial unionism, were determined to maintain the claims of their organizations to a portion of the auto workers. The device used to organize was the so-called federal labor union, with one chartered directly by the AFL for each plant. In theory, federal labor unions served as reservoirs in an organizing industry. Once all workers were enrolled, they would be divided by occupation among the craft unions.

The defects in this approach outnumbered its benefits. The federal labor unions had little independent power since officers were usually appointed, not elected. Most of the sums raised from dues went to the AFL; yet if the members struck, they were not entitled to support from the federation's strike fund unless the local had been in good standing for a year. In fact, the AFL collected more in dues from auto workers than it spent on their organization. Another problem was lack of coordination. Each federal labor union was tied to the AFL, but they had no tie among themselves. Not until June 1934 was a national council set up, and only in August 1935 was an international union of auto workers created under AFL auspices.

Furthermore, the AFL's leadership in auto was ineffective. Collins had no experience in the industry, and his successor, Francis Dillon, had little. Collins was convinced that failure was inevitable, and Dillon was almost as pessimistic. As late as March 1935, when auto workers by the hundreds of thousands had demonstrated their desire for a militant organization that could challenge the companies, Dillon warned that "above all else" they "must move cautiously." Thus the locals initiated those strikes that occurred without the approval of Collins or Dillon. Neither grasped that in a fluid situation the strike itself, the call to arms, was the most effective way to win the worker's loyalty. Auto workers were soon asking themselves what they gained by joining the AFL—other than risking their jobs.

The passage of the NIRA did not alter the manufacturers' opposition to unions. So many workers were laid off for economic reasons that it is impossible to determine the number of dismissals for union activity. Nevertheless, there is evidence of discrimination against union members and there is no question that workers feared they would be fired for joining. In fact, fear was the greatest deterrent to organization. Beginning in 1936, evidence of spying and other antiunion practices was developed by a subcommittee chaired by Senator Robert La Follette, Jr., of Wisconsin. The Ford Service Department spied on employees and kept track of their union activities. General Motors (GM) and Chrysler bought spy services from the Pinkerton National Detective Agency and the Corporation's Auxiliary Company. GM, Pinkerton's largest industrial client, spent approximately $1 million on labor espionage between January 1, 1934, and July 31, 1936, as well as large sums at other times. A Pinkerton agent who had contrived to win election to office in the Atlanta Chevrolet and Fisher Body local handed over union membership lists and other records to the company while the local, charging he had been laid off for union membership, was trying to get him reinstated in his job. The membership of a Flint amalgamated local of GM workers declined from 26,000 in February 1934 to 120 in 1936, primarily because of espionage and the threat of discriminatory layoff. "Perhaps nowhere," the committee concluded, was there a clearer relation between spying and infiltration, and the failure of unionization, "than in the automobile industry."

The AFL was not the only organization seeking auto workers. Among the others was the Mechanics Education Society of America (MESA), which had some success in organizing skilled workmen in GM's tool and die departments and in the independent shops that produced tooling for model changeovers. At the end of 1934 MESA claimed a membership of 38,000. Its growth was hampered, however, by a negligible appeal to production workers and by discord among leftist elements, centered on a vocal group of communists surrounding a Scots tool and die maker, John Anderson, the Communist party candidate for governor of Michigan in 1934 and later a stalwart communist in the UAW. The communist-led Auto Workers' Union (AWU) tried to seize the opportunity the depression afforded, but failed to establish a secure position among the workers. In December 1934 the AWU was dissolved. Henceforth, the communists' strategy was to "bore from within," joining noncommunist unions to influence their policies and actions. The early years of the depression also saw the birth of several other independent, short-lived labor organizations, such as the Automotive Industrial Workers' Association (AIWA), which had a following among Chrysler employees and eventually was absorbed by the UAW. From the AIWA came R. J. Thomas, president of the United Auto Workers from 1939 to 1946, and Richard Frankensteen, a vice-president.

Here and there a minor victory was won—enough to whet the appetite. In 1934 a federal labor union in Toledo became the most successful local of the time—and brought to notice George Addes, destined to be Reuther's most important UAW rival—by winning a strike against Electric Auto-Lite, an independent parts manufacturer. In the following year 2,300 Toledo workers shut down a Chevrolet transmission plant, forcing the corporation to stop production briefly in factories employing 32,000 workers. GM made concessions to resume production but refused to sign a contract. The company had the last word, however, when it later transferred half of the plant's machinery to other locations, eliminating many Toledo jobs.

Despite these efforts, in 1935, at the end of the New Deal's first phase, the auto workers were still unorganized and unprotected. No major manufacturer recognized a union or engaged in collective bargaining. The company's counterattacks against organizing campaigns had been successful. In Pontiac, Michigan, where three GM divisions employed about 12,000 workers, the Pontiac Motors federal labor union had only 20 active members, the Fisher Body local was smaller, and the GM Truck local had none at all. The AFL's federal labor unions declined from 100,000 members in 1933 to 23,000—only 5 percent of the wage earners in auto jobs—by 1935. The Ford Motor Company, which had totally ignored the collective bargaining promise of NIRA, remained off limits to organizers and had suffered no strikes.

In 1935 two issues that had plagued auto unions moved toward resolution. First, the legal sanction for unions was clarified and strengthened. In June the Supreme Court declared the National Industrial Recovery Act unconstitutional. It had proved an unsuccessful experiment, contributing little either to permanent unions or to recovery. To replace section 7(a) of NIRA, the collective bargaining provision, Congress passed the Wagner Act. Besides guaranteeing a right to collective bargaining for covered industries in general terms, the new law adopted the principle of majority rule, long familiar from political practice and democratic theory. If a union was selected by the majority of employees in a plant, it became the bargaining agent for all. The law established the National Labor Relations Board (NLRB) to conduct elections among competing unions and to investigate complaints against employers of unfair labor practices, such as discrimination against union members in hiring and firing, refusal to bargain, and interference with employees' rights and liberties. The NLRB, as a quasi-judicial body, could issue cease-and-desist orders to offending employers. In short, the law gave unions a legitimacy they had never before known, marking a profound and lasting shift in the federal government's relation to them. The Wagner Act strengthened labor's hand in organizing mass-production workers, but did not assure that result. Until a favorable Supreme Court decision in 1937, the act's constitutionality was uncertain. Although workers now had a better weapon in hand, backed by a more supportive national government, they still would have to rely mainly on themselves.

The second issue was the place of industrial unions in the labor movement. At the AFL's 1934 convention the champions of industrial organization, led by John L. Lewis, president of the

United Mine Workers, urged that new industrial internationals be chartered to replace the federal labor unions in the mass-production industries. Agreement was reached on chartering an auto workers' union, but the rights of craft unions to skilled workers in the industry were protected. A vague resolution defining the UAW's jurisdiction contained the seeds of future wrangles. These decisions were unacceptable to the auto workers themselves. At the first UAW convention in the summer of 1935, AFL President William Green protected the craft unions by refusing to allow the workers to choose their officers. When he announced that the unsatisfactory Francis Dillon would be the UAW-AFL's president, the organization, neither genuinely industrial nor democratic, was doomed. The AFL had lost the auto workers' confidence.

In October 1935 the issue of industrial unionism came to a head at the AFL's Atlantic City convention. Reuther, back in the country only a few weeks, attended as an observer. John L. Lewis again advocated the industrial unit as the basis for organizing in mass-production industries, but the delegates spurned his plea. On the convention floor, Lewis delivered a punch to the nose of the burly Carpenter's Union president, "Big Bill" Hutcheson, in response to an abusive remark. Then Lewis, the United Mine Workers, and the other industrial unions defied the AFL by setting up the Committee (later Congress) of Industrial Organizations (CIO). Although it would be two years before the break between AFL and CIO was formalized, they treated each other as rivals from the start. For the auto workers the way was now clear to organize an industrial union supported both by other unions and by a national organization with experienced, ambitious, and bold leadership.

The first generation of auto industry history, marked by extraordinary growth, high profits, and a quiescent work force, ended with the Great Depression. Henceforth the workers would demand a voice in their future, but just how they would gain that voice was still to be determined.

III

Birth of the
United Automobile Workers

WALTER AND VICTOR REUTHER returned to the United States at a crucial time. Despite the evident failure of the first campaign to organize an auto workers' union, the recent passage of the Wagner Act inspired workers to redouble their efforts. As the Roosevelt administration and progressive members of Congress moved toward a firmer commitment to unionism, they aroused a mounting, vocal, and well-financed opposition among business spokesmen. A battle was imminent that would determine industrial relations in the United States for years.

After a brief visit to their parents' home, the Reuthers hurried to Detroit to look for work and to renew contacts with unionists and fellow socialists, including their brother Roy, then an instructor in a workers' education program. Since neither could find a job with a car company, they suspected that they had been blacklisted. Using a pseudonym, Walter worked for two months for a large independent tooling company. Here again, the timing and circumstances of his firing suggest that union activity was the cause.

Lacking work in Detroit, the brothers had to turn elsewhere. A series of lectures in midwestern college towns on their experiences in the USSR and elsewhere was arranged through the League for Industrial Democracy. Just before Christmas they spoke at Brookwood Labor College in Katonah, New York, a socialist training school for union leaders and members, whose faculty Roy had joined. When Walter returned to Detroit, he declined an invitation to head a branch of the school planned for the Motor City, explaining that he preferred to play an active part in creating a union in the nation's leading industry.

Among the left-wing unionists Reuther met at the many meetings and conferences he attended was May Wolf, a young, attractive teacher in the Detroit schools and an active member of both the teachers' union and the Proletarian party, one of the small but militant Marxist organizations that then flourished in Detroit. Soon they began attending meetings together, crowding their courtship into the busy round of union and political activities. On March 15, 1936, the evening of their marriage, they drove to suburban Mount Clemens so that Reuther could deliver a speech at a union rally. Not long after, May Reuther resigned her teaching position to become her husband's secretary, because, she explained, that was the only way they could find time to be together.

Reuther's inability to find work in the auto industry made him ineligible for membership in the union, an embarrassing impediment for an ambitious organizer. His employment at Briggs and Ford years earlier would not suffice. Somehow he had to get into a union. Early in 1936 he was issued a card in the tiny UAW Local 86, which had been organized by socialist and communist workers at the Ternstedt Division of General Motors on Detroit's West Side. Opening a local to an unemployed but sympathetic outsider, though irregular, was not an unusual expedient. The organization had to recruit the necessary manpower for impending struggles even if this meant ignoring or bending the rules. As an unpaid volunteer organizer, Reuther had much to offer the UAW.

As the spring of 1936 approached, auto workers prepared for a convention of their union in South Bend, Indiana. Within the ranks there was overwhelming sentiment for an organization independent of AFL influence, with its officers selected by the delegates. Before the convention met, the UAW's vice-president, Homer Martin, and its secretary-treasurer, Ed Hall—both former auto workers—tried to maneuver the AFL's agent, President Francis Dillon, out of office. Although Dillon held on to his position and broke off relations with the other officers, he was not blind to the trend of events. When the convention met, he resigned and withdrew, leaving the delegates free to choose Homer Martin as the UAW's first auto worker president.

The 1936 convention marked the founding of an independent UAW. Although it remained affiliated with the AFL until that summer, it was no longer under AFL influence. Membership in the Congress of Industrial Organizations (CIO) followed a few months later. In addition to Martin, Ed Hall, Wyndham Mortimer, and Walter Wells were chosen as vice-presidents, and George Addes as secretary-treasurer.

Homer Martin, the new president, had worked briefly in the Kansas City Chevrolet factory. By training, experience, and inclination, however, he was a Baptist preacher. His congregation in Leeds, Missouri, had forced him to resign from the pulpit because of his prolabor convictions. Since his sympathies lay with the underdog, they told him, he could become one. An effective speaking style and a martyr's aura took him to the top of the infant UAW. The idioms and Biblical imagery of the evangelical sermon, which he had mastered, were readily adapted to the union's cause and struck home among the many southerners in the rank and file. This ability to stir their hearts proved a useful talent for the UAW's immediate task, but a shallow foundation on which to build effective leadership.

Most powerful among the other officers were Wyndham Mortimer and George Addes, each of whom already had important followings among the membership. Mortimer, a one-time machinist at White Motor Company in Cleveland, was an active unionist of long standing, whose loyalties stretched back to a boyhood in the Pennsylvania coal mines. Though never conceding membership in the Communist party, he followed its direction and line closely and was regarded as its leading UAW champion. George Addes, a metal polisher from the large Toledo local, had surfaced in a leading role in the Chevrolet strike of 1935. On the left but less tightly aligned there than Mortimer, he was a competent, honest manager of the union's internal business affairs and an effective politician.

Reuther attended the South Bend convention as Local 86's delegate. Six members were present at the meeting that selected him, and the entire treasury of $5 was turned over to meet his expenses. He hitchhiked to South Bend, stayed in the cheapest hotel he could find, and ate hamburgers—"and not many of them."

Reuther's humble circumstances were no obstacle to recognition. Surviving a challenge to his credentials on the ground that he had not been employed at the Ternstedt plant, Reuther won election to the general executive board, the union's governing body between conventions. When the list of nominees came before the convention, it was charged that he was barred by a constitutional requirement that no one could serve who had not been a member for two years—a provision that, as President Martin pointed out, excluded the bulk of the membership. Ruling that exceptions would be made for the time being, the president declared Reuther eligible, and he was elected. As informed delegates knew, it was Reuther's alignment with the left wing that both assured his election and sparked the opposition. Nevertheless, his selection demonstrated how quickly Reuther impressed contemporaries with his ability, as well as the opportunities for rapid advancement in the union in its early days.

Reuther gained the floor several times. During a debate on the number of vice-presidents the organization required, he argued for a larger number at smaller salaries. To expedite organizing and give representation to all the auto-producing areas, he thought, five vice-presidents rather than three should be authorized. Each should receive $3,000 a year, plus an expense account of $8 a day while traveling on union business. "We do not want to start creating big, fat jobs," Reuther said. "Let us start the salaries low, on the basis of what these men do." Even after he became the UAW's president, Reuther continued to oppose high salaries for union officials. On principle, he believed the standard of living of the leadership should not far exceed that of the rank and file.

The UAW was a characteristically youthful organization: hopeful, exciting, and unpredictable. Few of the auto workers had been in unions before, and few had been in organizations that utilized formal discussion. The union served as a school for its membership, training thousands in the ways of reaching agreement through debate and compromise. Those like the Reuthers who were at home with advocacy speaking and knew how meetings were conducted were valuable members and at an advantage. The small but well-organized and disciplined communist minority within the new unions of the 1930s rushed in to fill the leadership vacuum. Within a few years, however, the need for their services shrank and their influence declined as able rank-and-filers moved up through local offices and into the union's hierarchy.

The main task of the South Bend convention was to shape a membership drive. As a board member representing Michigan auto workers, Reuther had a fine opportunity to build a base in Detroit, the unorganized heart of the industry. The city's West Side was a vast, crowded field of parts and assembly plants, with only a handful of union members. GM's Cadillac Division, Fleetwood Fisher Body, and Ternstedt parts-manufacturing plants employed thousands. Several independent manufacturers were located there, particularly Kelsey-Hayes, a maker of wheels and brakes. Looming in the distance just outside the city was the mammoth Ford Rouge works. Altogether, the West Side including the Rouge employed 100,000 auto workers in 1936.

Reuther began work as soon as he returned from the convention. In September 1936 the UAW chartered Local 174, the West Side Local, an amalgam of units in Ford, Cadillac, Fleetwood, Ternstedt, and the independent plants. It started with fewer than one hundred members. Elected president, Reuther opened an office in a former bank building at 35th and Michigan Avenue, a streetcar transfer point for many Ford workers. Here and elsewhere, for the first time in Detroit, an auto workers' union was openly campaigning for members.

The sit-down strike quickly became the key weapon in the auto workers' organizing. The first significant victory came in early December at Midland Steel, an East Side frame manufacturer, where several hundred employees closed the plant with a sit-down strike. Used earlier by the Industrial Workers of the World, the sit-down was revived in the 1930s in France and Spain and, in the United States, at a rubber workers' strike in Akron. Its first use in the auto industry was at a Bendix plant in South Bend a few weeks before the Midland Steel strike.

A conventional strike relied on mass picketing to halt production. If a company chose to defy the strikers, however, scabs could be brought in past unguarded gates or rammed through the picket line by the police so that production could resume. These confrontations were costly to labor, often leading to arrests, lowered morale, unfavorable public opinion, and lost strikes.

The sit-down tactic shifted the balance toward the strikers. A contingent of determined workers, not necessarily a majority, seized a plant and refused to leave. Barriers were erected at doors and gates to guard against attempts to dislodge them by force. A supply of weapons—body hardware and the like in auto plants—was at hand to repel assault. If the police or management attempted to retake the plant by force, expensive machinery and inventory might be wrecked. The sit-down tended to enhance the strikers' morale and sense of solidarity. Scabs could not be brought in, and suspicions about the loyalty of one's fellows did not arise.

The use of a sit-down raised a legal and ethical question, since it violated the trespass law. Some union lawyers argued that the right to a job transcended the property right protected by trespass, a claim rejected by the Supreme Court in 1941. Until then a haze of uncertainty surrounded sit-downs, but most people considered them illegal.

The charge of illegality, however, was tempered by two

considerations. One was the widely, though not universally, accepted belief that the times required bold measures. Roosevelt's New Deal, backed by the electorate, stood for a more powerful role for labor, one that labor itself must in part establish. Probably no substantial redistribution of power could take place without illegal incidents. Furthermore, although the Wagner Act promised collective bargaining, that law was still untested. Most auto workers, with reason, expected that employers would defy or evade it. Did one party's defiance or evasion of a law justify disobedience of a different law by another party? Auto workers felt that it did. To complicate matters further, company refusal to acknowledge the right of unions to exist and represent employees led to a vicious circle. Unless a union proved its strength, it had little claim on the workers' loyalty. Without their loyalty, it could not bring about or win bargaining elections. The sit-down broke the impasse by demonstrating the union's strength.

The sit-downs established the limits of the American public's tolerance for extraordinary action in implementing change. Once unions won recognition in 1937, the sit-down was discarded. Thus, even before the Supreme Court ruled in 1941 that sit-down strikes were illegal, they had ceased to be used.

The Kelsey-Hayes strike of December 1936, two weeks before the famous sit-down of Chevrolet workers in Flint, was a classic demonstration of the technique. Throughout the fall Reuther and other organizers signed up Kelsey-Hayes workers. Progress was slow, however, since most workers still feared being fired for union membership. Gradually, a reliable nucleus was formed in one department of the company. Victor Reuther, then working for a Friends' peace group in the East, received a telegram from Walter and Roy: "If you are interested in the organizing of auto workers, come immediately back to Detroit." He left the same day and was hired at Kelsey-Hayes as a punch press operator. His wife went to work in the office of Local 174, where her knowledge of Polish was useful. The plant had been infiltrated successfully.

Kelsey-Hayes, which employed about five thousand workers

in two plants, was not large enough to be unwieldy. Most of its products were sold to Ford. A successful strike there was bound to draw the attention of a more important target—the many thousands of Ford workers.

Planning proceeded for a strike in behalf of union recognition, higher wages, a grievance procedure, and improved working conditions. How could the strike be launched with sufficient worker support to ensure success? One woman who worked in the shop, a union member, had fainted on the line a few months before. This had been attributed to the speedup, a major complaint of Kelsey-Hayes workers. Perhaps she could faint again. When she readily agreed, word was spread quietly among a few trusted union members that her collapse would signal the beginning of the strike. It was timed to occur just before a change in shifts so that the maximum number of workers would be exposed. Once the strike began, Reuther was to remain at union headquarters until contacted for talks by management. On December 10, 1936, twenty minutes before the day shift ended, the woman fainted on schedule. Victor Reuther pulled the main switch to stop the line, and unionists ran shouting through the factory, relaying the woman's story.

Within moments a huge crowd milled around waiting for a lead. When Victor mounted a packing crate for a speech, the company's personnel director came over and tugged at his trouser leg. "What are you doing? What are you doing?" he asked. Victor explained that he was telling the workers why they needed a union. "Get back to work," said the personnel director.

"No," Victor answered, "We'll not get back to work. If you want us to get back to work, you will sit down with Walter Reuther and an elected committee."

"Who in the hell is Reuther?"

"He's the president of our union." Victor gave him Walter's number, and soon the director was on the phone.

"Is your name Reuther?"

"Yes."

"I want you to tell these men to get back to work."

"Where are you?" asked Reuther.

"I'm inside the plant."

"But I'm outside the plant and can't tell anybody to get back to work as long as I'm out here. Send a car over to pick me up and take me into the plant and I'll talk to the guys."

Walter replaced Victor on the crate and launched into a speech in behalf of the union. The distraught personnel man grabbed his leg. "What the hell is this?" he asked. "You're supposed to tell them to go back to work."

"I can't tell them to do anything," Reuther replied, "until I first get them organized."

For a few days Kelsey-Hayes management delayed the drive. Wage increases were offered to some workers in return for abandoning the union. The employer's attempt to breathe life into a moribund company union was forestalled when UAW members marched into its meeting, took it over, and voted to disband. When management refused to bargain, the sit-down began. About five hundred workers remained inside two Kelsey-Hayes plants. Support was quickly organized to put up picket lines that would give security to the sit-downers on the inside and supply them with food and other necessities. Strike bulletins were issued and press briefings held.

Ford's reliance on Kelsey-Hayes caused the strike's effects to spread quickly. Threatened with a production halt because of parts shortages, Ford planned to remove dies from Kelsey-Hayes and install them in the Rouge. The workers quickly counterattacked by erecting heavy barriers, constructed of crates and dollies filled with auto parts, at the gates. Auto workers from other plants gathered by the thousands on the picket lines. The Ford plan was blocked.

With several thousand workers laid off, Ford pressured Kelsey-Hayes to yield by threatening to buy elsewhere. The settlement came on Christmas Eve. The main items were a general wage increase, a guaranteed minimum of 75 cents an hour, and equal pay for equal work for women. The union also gained a shop steward system for grievances and acceptance of seniority for regulating layoffs and recalls.

The strikers had won. It was the first major victory for auto workers on the West Side and one of the earliest in the city. As often happened, once a union had demonstrated strength and militance, membership soared. Local 174 grew from 78 members to 3,000 within a few days; in another year, it had increased to over 35,000. The Kelsey-Hayes strike was the turning point on the West Side and also a turning point for Reuther, who had demonstrated his ability to plan a campaign and mobilize and lead workers in industrial combat. Although the strike was a team effort, as president of the union and chief negotiator, Reuther received much of the credit. Local 174 gave him a large and loyal base within the UAW.

The decisive struggle began a few days later with General Motors, the industry's giant. If the UAW could bring GM workers into the union, successfully strike the corporation, and gain recognition, then the organization of the entire industry was possible. The UAW began to plan an assault on the Chevrolet Division, the heart of GM's empire.

Reuther played only a small part in the great Flint sit-down, which began on December 30, 1936, and lasted until February 11, 1937. Roy and Victor were key figures, however. With a 1930 population of 156,492, Flint was a company town in which 80 percent of the families depended on General Motors for their living. The Chevrolet and Buick Divisions, Fisher Body, and AC Spark Plug conducted major manufacturing and assembly operations. The city government and newspaper reflected the corporation's interests. Prior to the sit-down, the UAW had organized only a small and shifting fraction of GM workers against the corporation's devastating countertactics. Union leaders were fired and meetings infiltrated by spies. A GM official offhandedly confessed to the La Follette committee that "there was a very natural growth" of espionage in Flint as the union's threat mounted. Although Walter Reuther was not directly involved in Flint, GM assigned a spy to report on his activities.

For months, UAW organizers, including Roy Reuther, had been planning an eventual strike in Flint, but the strike broke out spontaneously. In November 1936 the election of a Democrat, Frank Murphy, as Michigan's governor assured the auto workers of sympathy and restraint in Lansing. Murphy took office on January 1, 1937. By refusing to allow the use of force to expel the strikers, he became the key figure in preventing loss of life and in pressuring the corporation to bargain.

The strike began when the union's ability to protect its members' jobs and their right to belong to the union were put to the test. At Fisher Body No. 2 on the morning of December 30, 50 workers protested against the corporation's disciplining of three inspectors who had refused to withdraw from the union when management, which considered them supervisors, ordered them to do so. The plant employed about 1,000 workers, who built 450 Chevrolet bodies a day. That evening Fisher Body No. 1, which employed about 7,300 workers and produced 1,400 bodies a day for Buick, was closed by a sit-down when the local UAW leadership ordered a strike to prevent the corporation from shipping body dies to plants outside Flint that had fewer union members. The corporation took the position that, although it was always prepared to discuss grievances with its employees, there could be no talks so long as the two plants were occupied.

At first GM made no effort to dislodge the sit-downers; but on January 11, in a confrontation the workers called the "Battle of the Running Bulls," the corporation tried to break the strike. That evening about thirty Flint policemen attacked Fisher Body No. 2 with tear gas. They were met with a barrage of car door hinges and other body hardware, rocks, bottles, and blasts of water from high-pressure hoses. When the wind blew the tear gas back toward the police, they began to retreat; but some drew their pistols and fired into the strikers' ranks. Fourteen strikers and sympathizers were wounded, nearly all by gunshots, as were nine policemen and the sheriff and a deputy sheriff of Genesee County who were struck by missiles. By this time thousands of spectators lined the streets, and the police fired gas bombs into the crowd, provoking another bombardment of rocks. Reforming and reinforcing their lines, they launched a second gas attack on the plants and the pickets that continued until after midnight. The strikers' repulse of the attack strengthened their resolve, but it also brought troops to Flint. Informed that order had collapsed, Governor Murphy sent in the National Guard to keep the two sides apart. He then assumed the role of mediator.

By this time strikes had broken out at other GM plants in Ohio, Indiana, Wisconsin, and Missouri. On January 8, Reuther called a sit-down at Cadillac's West Side Detroit plant. A few days later, following the Battle of the Running Bulls, that strike was extended to the nearby Fleetwood plant of Fisher Body. The Detroit sit-downers evacuated these plants on January 15, but picket lines maintained the strike. By the end of January, fifty GM plants with more than 125,000 employees were closed either by strikes or by parts shortages. Although the corporation had maintained production of some of its lines, its share of the market began to drop. Nevertheless, it was not prepared to yield.

The UAW seized the initiative on February 1, when it extended the sit-down to a key Flint plant, Chevrolet No. 4, which manufactured all Chevrolet engines. The union's tactics are celebrated in labor history. The two UAW men in charge, Bob Travis and Roy Reuther, took advantage of company spies within the union's ranks. Word was leaked that the union planned to seize a different plant, Chevrolet No. 9. As expected, GM massed its plant guards there, along with Flint police and sheriff's deputies. Only a handful of loyalists were told that Chevy No. 4 was the target. As the day shift ended in mid-afternoon, UAW workers in No. 9 called for a strike and began to shut down the machines. Fighting broke out both inside and outside the plant, with the unionists getting the worst of it. Most of those involved believed their effort had failed. Meanwhile, however, a union contingent of a few hundred seized Chevy No. 4 from a depleted force of company guards, supervisory personnel, and a larger number of employees loyal to the company. As company police entered, they came under a hail of pistons, connecting rods, and other engine parts. When the strikers won control of the plant, they barricaded the entrances with heavy crates and other parts containers. Walter Reuther, with a force from the West Side local and several hundred more from Detroit and Toledo, helped out. No one was killed, but there were many injuries on both sides. The seizure of Chevy 4 shut down Chevrolet production completely, exerting an irresistible pressure on the corporation to bargain.

The negotiations that led to settlement of the strike began in Detroit on February 3, with John L. Lewis, the CIO chief, and Governor Frank Murphy in the leading roles. GM had refused to negotiate until the plants were evacuated but found a pretext for abandoning that position when President Roosevelt requested the corporation to begin discussions. The basic issue was union recognition. Initially the UAW sought the exclusive right to bargain for all employees. GM pointed out that only a minority of its workers were union members and maintained that the great majority opposed UAW representation. When negotiations began, the union offered a concession, asking that it be granted bargaining rights in the twenty plants on strike. Once this was granted, it said, operations could be resumed and the remaining issues settled in collective bargaining. It also insisted that the strikers be allowed to return to their jobs without penalty.

For several days the corporation refused to make important concessions, while Governor Murphy, under increasing pressure, considered ways of forcing the strikers from the plants. After some concessions on both sides, agreement was announced on February 11. Although the UAW did not obtain an express pledge of exclusive representation, GM promised that for six months the corporation would not "bargain with or enter into agreements with any other union or representative of employees of plants on strike." The union's position on other issues prevailed, with the corporation promising to bargain on the original demands.

Several considerations determined the corporation's decision to conclude the strike on terms it had previously rejected. Governor Murphy's refusal to put government power at the company's disposal tied GM's hands. His restraint in using force—he said he would not go down in history as "Bloody

Murphy"—reduced the chance of loss of life and limited GM's options. Behind the scenes, the administration in Washington was exerting pressure for a settlement. Most important, however, was the determination of the strikers themselves and the support they received from their families and their union brothers and sisters. By seizing key strong points in GM's vast and interdependent collection of properties, they crippled its production and earning power. In the first ten days of February—while Ford and Chrysler, which hated unions but loved profits, continued to produce and sell cars—the giant of the industry built only 151 vehicles in the United States. During the strike, the corporation lost the production of 280,000 cars. The economy was improving in the early months of 1937, and demand was strong. GM was losing sales it could not regain.

In the last analysis, the issue in the GM strike and in the industrial union movement of the 1930s was an attack on the arbitrary, excessive power of employers—an attack in behalf of social justice and human dignity. Among auto workers, still relatively better paid than most other employees, wages were not the burning question. "I ain't got no kick on wages," a Flint man told a reporter, "but I just don't like to be drove." The rights to fair treatment from supervisors, to some influence on working conditions, and to the job security afforded by seniority were more important to auto workers than strictly monetary issues. A Midland Steel striker summed it up: "When you belong to a union, the foreman can't screw you."

Although Walter Reuther did not play a major role in the Flint sit-down, the strike enhanced his standing in the union. The Cadillac and Fleetwood strikes were important, if secondary, conflicts that closed down production of the top GM line. Several times Reuther rallied squadrons of Detroit workers for picket line or other support duty in Flint. The ability of the UAW to mobilize a "strategic reserve" from Michigan and Ohio auto cities made a significant contribution to victory.

Most important, however, was Reuther's association with Roy and Victor, two of the strike's most vocal and active leaders. Along with Bob Travis, Roy was a leading tactician as well as a strong speaker in union meetings and on the picket line. He had started organizing in Flint well before the strike began and was trusted and liked by the auto workers. In one dramatic incident, he exposed a GM spy at a union meeting, producing an uproar from which the spy was fortunate to escape unharmed. Victor was the UAW's public voice. For most of the strike he manned its sound truck, a crucial piece of equipment, and in the thick of the fight relayed orders to sit-downers and pickets and rallied the troops with the martial songs of the labor movement played over the loudspeakers. The Reuther name spread throughout the union, the industry, and even the nation. During the Kelsey-Hayes strike, when Walter was negotiating for Local 174, Victor was agitating in the plant, and Roy was making headlines in Flint, a distraught company official asked Walter, "How many of you damn Reuthers are there?" They seemed to be everywhere.

The UAW victory at Flint was decisive for the establishment of industrial unionism. If the young, untried UAW could bring the "most powerful industrial aggregation" in the country to terms, then industrial unionism was here to stay. A *New York Times* headline was close to the truth when it said, "Future of C.I.O. Hangs on Auto Strike Result."

With the momentum generated by its victory over GM, the UAW stormed ahead. Strikes broke out everywhere in Detroit. A *Detroit News* reporter observed that "sitting down has replaced baseball as the national pastime, and sitter-downers clutter up the landscape in every direction." In March a strike began at Chrysler, then the industry's second-largest firm in sales. The sit-downers evacuated the plants in return for a company promise not to resume production during negotiations. Workers and their wives walked the picket line singing "Dollars from Chrysler" to the tune of "Pennies from Heaven," the most popular song of the day. The strike, which lasted a month, brought recognition of the union and other gains. Many other parts and vehicle manufacturers in Detroit and elsewhere were brought into line in the spring and summer of 1937. The UAW was on its way.

When the sit-downers marched out of the Cadillac and Fleetwood factories only two miles from the Rouge plant, they carried a banner hopefully proclaiming "Today GM—Tomorrow Ford." Everyone knew that Ford would be tough. Although the Supreme Court, in April 1937, upheld the constitutionality of the collective bargaining guarantee in the Wagner Act, Henry Ford deserved his reputation for stubbornly going his own way despite government laws and employee wishes. At the beginning of the UAW's drive, he announced flatly that "we'll never recognize the United Automobile Workers Union or any other union."

Ford knew how to fight. From 1937 to 1941, over four thousand Ford workers suspected of union membership were fired. The Ford Service Department, under the redoubtable Harry Bennett, was the world's largest and most brutal plant police force. Nevertheless, a nucleus of union members worked in Ford factories, and the UAW was eager for battle. Homer Martin's floundering as president put the union's leadership up for grabs. Whoever gained credit for organizing Ford would likely be Martin's successor.

The campaign began in April 1937. A few Ford workers met secretly with union officials to devise tactics. For the sake of security, inconspicuous UAW offices were opened in areas far from the Ford plant. Bulletins and leaflets were issued in English, Polish, Serbo-Croatian, and other languages. With memories of the lives lost in the Hunger March still fresh, soliciting members seemed risky; but the union had to come into the open to let the Ford workers know it did not fear their employer.

Reuther's first scheme, though safe, was ineffective. He and Vic, the operator of the Flint sound truck, hired an airplane with amplification equipment and, shouting slogans, circled the Rouge plant. Their cries were drowned out by the roar of the engine and carried away by the wind. Richard Frankensteen, a UAW vice-president, proposed to sponsor a radio broadcast by the Detroit Symphony Orchestra, in imitation of Ford's presentation of the orchestra's Sunday evening radio program. Reuther, pointing out that Ford workers were not known for their devotion to classical music, ridiculed the idea, which was voted down by the executive board. Other ideas showed more promise, however. Union members and sympathizers, for example, signed up for the visitors' tour of the Rouge plant and, once in among the workers, donned union caps and flashed small signs reading, "Get Wise—Organize."

Handbill distribution was a time-honored method of spreading the union message. On May 26, 1937, Reuther, along with Frankensteen and Bill McKie, a fired Ford worker and a communist, organized a massive handbill distribution at the gates of the Rouge plant. The single-sheet leaflet consisted of quotes from the Wagner Act and an appeal to join the union. Hundreds of volunteers, including many women, assembled. Reuther, Frankensteen, and a few others arrived early at Gate 4, where an elevated footbridge crossed the road. In the "Battle of the Overpass" that followed, Ford brutality was amply demonstrated. Once on the bridge, the unionists were surrounded and severely beaten by a gang of forty Ford thugs. As Walter recalled:

> The men . . . picked me up about eight different times and threw me down on my back on the concrete and while I was on the ground, they kicked me in the face, head and other parts of my body. . . . Finally they got me next to Dick who was lying on the bridge and with both of us together they kicked me again and then picked me up and threw me down the first flight of stairs. I lay there and they picked me up and began to kick me down the total flight of steps.

Frankensteen, who fought back, was badly battered. Others, including some of the women, were beaten, one man suffering a broken back. Nearby police did nothing to stop the attack, although the UAW had received a permit for leaflet distribution. The attack was fully documented by the press, and a *Detroit News* photographer won the Pulitzer Prize for a set of photos that were republished in *Time* and throughout the world. Painful as it was, creating martyrs would ultimately help the cause. As *Time* commented, following a detailed description, "it looked very much as if that brutal beating might hurt Henry Ford as much as it hurt Richard Frankensteen."

The campaign to organize Ford bogged down, almost as much because of internal union disputes and quarreling leaders as because of Ford's opposition. Smarting under unfavorable publicity, Ford took care to avoid assault and battery but otherwise did not relent. Nevertheless, more leaflets were handed out. Reuther distributed 200,000 copies of Upton Sinclair's muckraking novel about Ford, *The Flivver King*. As part of a strategy to shore up his crumbling presidency, Martin, hoping to slow Reuther's rise in the union, appointed Frankensteen director of the Ford organizing drive. Reuther remained active in the campaign, however.

Despite the failure to crack Ford on the first try, the UAW grew rapidly, reaching 300,000 members by the end of 1937. It seemed destined to become a leading American union—perhaps, as CIO president John L. Lewis suggested, labor's preeminent organization. The road to permanence and power was longer than many expected, however. The companies remained hostile. Public opinion, soured by sit-downs and unauthorized wildcat strikes, turned less sympathetic. Moreover, success posed its own question: With the UAW now established, who would be in control? For ten years, through the rest of the depression and World War II, the union was racked by strife over direction and leadership. Rival factions, fed on differing ideologies and the conflicting ambitions of determined men, created a series of crises that jeopardized the UAW's existence.

IV

Internecine Struggles

INTERNAL DIVISIONS almost destroyed the UAW between the sit-down of 1937 and the outbreak of World War II in 1941. Controversies swirled around issues, ideologies, politics, and individuals. Homer Martin, the former preacher, was out of his depth as UAW president, something nearly everyone except him soon realized. Distrusting Martin's judgment and vanity, John L. Lewis had deftly replaced him as the UAW's negotiator during the GM sit-down strike by sending the president on a speaking tour of distant locals. Consequently, a chagrined Martin learned of the settlement from the newspapers while changing trains in Chicago. As other unionists made names for themselves, Martin tried to shore up his deteriorating position by exiling potential rivals. The Reuthers were important enough to be a target. He transferred Roy and Vic out of Flint to less important manufacturing cities before the sit-down ended; and other battle-tested leaders of that struggle, such as Bob Travis, were demoted. Since Walter, as president of a local, held no staff position in the international union, he was for the time being less vulnerable to Martin's attack.

In the politicized atmosphere of the New Deal labor movement, maneuvering for power and position went on constantly since the stakes—control of working class institutions—were high. Desperate for support and advice, Martin entered into a strange alliance. Convinced that the Stalinist communists, defenders of everything Russian, were the greatest threat to his control, he accepted the services of Jay Lovestone, head of a tiny but militantly anti-Stalinist sect of ex-Communists. Lovestone, once secretary of the American Communist party, had been dismissed on Stalin's orders for believing that he was Stalin's equal in the party hierarchy. No quitter, Lovestone launched his own organization, the Communist party of the USA (Opposition), and engaged in a ceaseless settling of scores with his enemies. The UAW became one of his battlegrounds. "The filthy Stalinist lice," he snarled, "are crawling all over the UAW; they must be stamped out!"

Comfortable only as a power behind the throne, Lovestone used his influence over Martin to place his own followers in key staff positions. Well-known Lovestoneites received appointments as UAW research director, as administrative assistant to the president, as head of the women's auxiliary, and as organizers. With only a minuscule following in the plants, the Lovestone faction hoped to run the UAW from the top in order to purge the hated Stalinists.

Since no single element was large or strong enough to control the UAW, rival coalitions quickly formed. Around Martin gathered those who came to be known as the Progressive Caucus, actually situated on the right in the political spectrum. Martin had a genuine, if limited, following within the union, especially in those plants in Flint and auto cities outside of Michigan where southern-born workers warmed to his oratory. This support steadily diminished, however, as evidence mounted of his administrative bumbling and personal and political inadequacy. The heart of the Progressive Caucus was the following of vice-president Richard Frankensteen, a burly, capable organizer and an ambitious, pragmatic politician. His strength lay primarily in the big Chrysler locals in Detroit. Expediency brought a few others into the caucus, including a small band of Trotskyites. Lovestone's followers, the Progressives' intellectual lights, were so consumed with an anti-Stalinist and anti–Popular Front passion that anticommunism became the Progressive Caucus's rallying cry.

A left-wing opposition to Martin emerged, known as the Unity Caucus, made up of the Reuthers, other socialists and independent leftists, the Communists, and a large nonideological element of the rank and file. Socialists formed a significant element in the UAW; but their political position was undermined as President Roosevelt, Governor Murphy, and other liberal Democrats, moving to the left, brought vital support to labor. Many, like Reuther, chose not to identify with the Democratic party, whose racist southern wing was one of several elements they could not stomach. They could not resist the practical advantages of an alignment with a major party that had given indispensable aid to labor, however; nor could they ignore Roosevelt's growing popularity with the rank and file. In his "last hurrah" as a political socialist, Reuther ran for a seat on the Detroit Common Council in the fall of 1937 on a Socialist-backed slate in the officially nonpartisan election. None of those on the slate was elected, including its mayoral candidate, although Reuther and several others ran strong races. It was to be his only try for political office.

Reuther's political loyalties became an issue in 1938, when he endorsed the Democrat Frank Murphy for reelection as governor and took the lead in forming and financing a UAW Political Action Committee for Murphy's support, even though the Socialist party was running a candidate in the election. Since he supported the candidate of a different party, Reuther submitted his resignation to the Socialist party but was persuaded to withdraw it by party officials who believed, pragmatically, that a socialist labor leader who refused to support the party's candidate was better than no socialist labor leader at all. In 1939 Reuther quietly resigned from the party. Henceforth, though nominally independent, he regularly supported New Deal Democrats in national and state elections. Although he ceased to be a member of the Socialist party, his conception of the union as a politically active, reformist organization and of government's responsibility to experiment with collective approaches to solving public problems continued to be inspired by democratic socialist ideals.

The other important element in the Unity Caucus consisted of the communists and their allies. For them, capitalism's depression crisis was the foreordained opportunity to advance the class struggle and establish positions of strength within the emboldened institutions of the working class. Although there is little evidence that rank-and-file auto workers were drawn to communism's revolutionary goals, a strong sense of class differences and of conflicting class interests with owners and management, as well as an appreciation of militant rhetoric and tactics, forged a tie between many ordinary workers and communist spokesmen. Communist party membership among auto workers, never large, ranged from 630 in 1935 to 1,100 in 1939. Backing for the party's positions and of its leadership cadres was far greater than these meager figures indicate; but beyond the core of party members and close fellow travelers, the commitment became increasingly shallow. Communist strength was located in the larger auto cities like Detroit, Cleveland, and Milwaukee, where it was centered in locals with either Communist or fellow-traveling officers.

Reuther's relation to the communists in 1935–1938 continued to rest on the Popular Front principle—the unity of the left against its common enemies. To many UAW noncommunists, he was at least a fellow traveler and perhaps a full-fledged communist. After all, he was the only UAW leader who had lived and worked in the Soviet Union, and he had openly cooperated with known communists within the UAW. The West Side Local 174, of which he was president, employed left-wingers, including communists, in staff positions, sponsored performances of Clifford Odets's revolutionary drama *Waiting for Lefty*, and conducted other educational and cultural activities with a left orientation.

Politicians and rival labor leaders bent on discrediting the CIO added to the suspicion. In 1938 Reuther was one of more than three hundred CIO figures named in the first hearings of the Dies committee, the predecessor of the House Un-American Activities Committee, as Communists or Communist sympathizers. The undocumented charges, which came mainly from an AFL official, were swallowed whole by the credulous. Although there is no question that Reuther cooperated with the Communists for several years, there is no conclusive evidence that he ever was or wished to be a member of the party.

Martin's struggle to retain control of the UAW followed a shifting but ever downward course. Minor though irritating and costly sit-down strikes—so-called quickies—broke out in many GM plants following the 1937 settlement—170 between March and June alone, according to GM. Since the settlement included no adequate procedure for resolving grievances, the quickie was resorted to for that purpose. Furthermore, since workers wanted to flex their new muscles, whereas foremen and other plant officials were reluctant to concede that any change had taken place, tempers were short on both sides. Although these sit-downs had little if anything to do with union politics, Martin chose to interpret them as efforts by the communists to embarrass him. Once he foolishly agreed to a unilateral GM proposal to discipline workers who engaged in unauthorized strikes. This allowed his opponents to charge him with betraying the workers.

The first test of strength between the Progressive and Unity camps came in a fractious convention in Milwaukee in August 1937, one of the most disorderly meetings in union history. Speakers, including President Martin, were repeatedly interrupted by boos, shouts, and demonstrations. At one point delegates were so incensed over Martin's dictatorial mismanagement of a key vote on a credentials dispute that he was unable to continue until Reuther and Addes pleaded with their Unity followers to permit the president to proceed. In order to curb Martin's reckless use of power, the Unity Caucus proposed a series of constitutional amendments to decentralize authority and protect local autonomy and democratic procedures. The election of officers, as usual the cause of the greatest disturbances, was finally resolved by a compromise pushed through by John L. Lewis, which left Martin in the presidency

The communists engineered the breakup of the Unity Caucus by wooing Richard Frankensteen, the powerful UAW vice-president, and discarding Reuther. From a political standpoint, Frankensteen, who had once thought highly of Father Coughlin, the demagogic, anti-Roosevelt "radio priest," had little in common with the communists except a desire for power. That sufficed to bring them together, however. The disruption of the caucus came at the founding convention of the Michigan CIO in April 1938. The Unity Caucus had agreed to support Victor Reuther for secretary-treasurer of the organization against Richard T. Leonard, Frankensteen's ally and the Progressive Caucus candidate. At the last moment, the communist delegates were instructed to switch their votes to Leonard, who then won easily. Just before the vote Reuther discovered the plot and warned his new enemies: "If you carry through this double-cross, then count me on the other side, not only in this fight, but from here on out!" A tough politician, he never forgot and never forgave.

With Frankensteen allied with the communists, Homer Martin was dangerously isolated. An alignment with Reuther, now adrift, would have made tactical sense; but Martin lacked the survival instinct necessary for such a bold, subtle stroke. He chose instead to launch a frontal attack on his enemies, suspending George Addes, the secretary-treasurer, and four of the five UAW vice-presidents. In protest, six members of the executive board, including Reuther, refused to attend further meetings and thereupon were suspended. Martin trumped up charges against the suspended officers, and his rump board expelled four of them. The anti-Martinites, now constituting a great majority of the union and fearful for its survival, demanded that John L. Lewis intervene. Reuther urged Lewis to ask Martin to call a special convention. If, as was expected, he refused, the CIO would issue the call. Lewis, however, feared that a convention would turn into a riot. Instead he sent his most trusted CIO lieutenants—Philip Murray, head of the steelworkers' union, and Sidney Hillman, president of the Amalgamated Clothing Workers—to straighten things out. In effect, they temporarily took over the UAW by requiring reinstatement of the expelled and suspended officers and by establishing a joint committee under their guidance to decide all disputes. Martin, desperate, contacted both the scorned AFL and the Ford Motor Company without the board's knowledge, apparently intending to take the UAW out of the CIO and to negotiate a contract with Ford. By early 1939 the UAW was split between the Martin group and the UAW-CIO. Each called a special convention to assert its control over the union.

The two sides fought it out, sometimes literally, in the UAW locals, where the election of delegates would decide the UAW's future. Martin's desertion of the CIO cost him heavily, since the auto workers could easily recall the AFL's failures before the CIO came on the scene. His sparsely attended convention in Detroit demonstrated that Martin had ceased to be a major force, but it authorized affiliation of his branch of the UAW with the AFL.

The mood of the UAW-CIO's Cleveland convention was hopeful. With the factions still in disarray, Sidney Hillman, Lewis's representative, managed the proceedings. Reuther launched a strong attack on Frankensteen, excoriating his mishandling of the Ford organizing drive and questioning his capacity for leadership. The most vigorous conflict was, as usual, over the election of officers. The communists, with about fifty delegates and a larger pool of supporters, reached the peak of their UAW influence. Some writers have claimed that they could have controlled the presidential election, bringing in Addes or even the more controversial Mortimer; but the claim appears weak considering that Mortimer lost his vice-presidency and that the representation of communist sympathizers on the executive board declined. In the end, Hillman and Murray put through a shrewd compromise. R. J. Thomas, the last of the union's officers to abandon Martin and still influential with elements sympathetic to him, was put forward as president. Addes was reelected as secretary-treasurer; the vice-presidencies, the focus of factional conflict, were simply abolished.

The choice of Thomas strengthened the UAW-CIO's hand in its battle with Homer Martin and the AFL. Thomas was not allied with any of the left-wing factions. He was an auto worker who had come into the union in its earliest days at Chrysler with the tastes and habits of the rank and file. He spoke the language of the shop, chewed tobacco, played poker, and liked to have a beer in the bars near the Chrysler plant on East Jefferson in Detroit. As one historian wrote, Thomas "had no intellectual or leadership qualifications for the presidency of the UAW. But he was loyal, honest, big-hearted, stable, and colorless, all wildly attractive characteristics after Homer Martin."

Reuther emerged from the convention with an important new responsibility. Thomas offered, and he accepted, the post of director of the General Motors Department. With the locals in many GM plants divided between pro- and anti-Martin factions, the corporation had taken the position that it was not obliged to deal with either. The fragmented GM locals would have to be rebuilt in the face of both Martin's and the company's opposition—almost the same as starting over. Although the job was a big one with no certain outcome, by the same token, if Reuther met the challenge, his standing in the union would be greatly enhanced.

To reestablish the UAW-CIO, several tactical routes were available. The first was a conventional strike of production workers. Since the car market was still depressed, however, and GM therefore had little need for uninterrupted production, a strike would be long and costly. The layoffs of 1938 had exhausted many workers' savings, and the union had no strike fund. A sit-down was out of the question, since public opinion would no longer tolerate it and Michigan's Republican governor would be hostile. Another option was to follow the electoral procedures of the Wagner Act, but this course also had disadvantages. The National Labor Relations Board was bogged down in disputes. The process was bound to be time consuming since

GM would fight it at every step, but the UAW-CIO needed an immediate victory over both Martin's union and the car makers.

Reuther devised an alternative plan that revealed striking gifts for analysis and bold execution. He proposed to maximize pressure on the corporation while minimizing the risk and cost to the workers by calling a strike of GM tool and die makers, but not of production workers. Tools and dies were being completed for the 1940 models, which the corporation was counting on to bring it out of the recession. If the tool and die makers struck, most workers, still producing the 1939 models, would continue to earn wages while the corporation's competitive prospects deteriorated. In addition, unemployment compensation had recently gone into operation in Michigan. If the strike continued beyond the 1939 model run, with layoffs of production workers, they would become eligible for payments.

Homer Martin tried to beat Reuther to the punch by calling strikes at GM assembly plants in Flint and Saginaw. UAW-CIO workers ignored the AFL picket lines, however, and the plants continued to operate. Martin succeeded only in demonstrating his weakness. Still, the Reuther or strategy strike, as it was called, was a gamble. The union was internally divided, and GM refused to recognize either the Martin or the Thomas-Reuther group as the holder of a legal contract. The communists, although they dared not oppose the strike openly, did not want a Reuther victory. Some of the rank and file were hostile, indifferent, or pessimistic. In the absence of either a dues checkoff or a union shop that would require workers to join the union, only 8 percent of the workers in the plants organized by the UAW were paying dues when the strike began. If the strike flopped, the union would suffer a devastating setback.

Reuther planned the preliminary rounds carefully. The corporation was asked to enter negotiations but refused on the grounds that it was uncertain whom, if anyone, the UAW-CIO represented. Strike votes at eight GM tool and die shops showed more than 90 percent ready to go out. Another decision was to begin the strike in only the most militant shops and then, as GM held out, escalate to others that would not lead but were prepared to follow. *Time* called this a "new and shrewdly conceived" technique, "not unlike amputating one finger at a time to cripple a hand."

The strike began on July 5, 1939. Fisher 21 in Detroit, which made welding tools and fixtures, was the first to go. By the next day, five shops were closed, including Fisher 23, the largest tool and die facility in the world with 1,600 employees, and the Detroit die shop of Chevrolet Gear and Axle. The latter's 800 tool and die strikers were joined on the picket lines by 2,500 production workers, a demonstration of support by those who stood to realize no immediate gain. Ultimately the strike spread to eleven shops, almost completely stalling GM's preparations for the 1940 models.

Reuther orchestrated activities to mobilize union and public support. A demonstration at GM headquarters brought out 10,000 production workers, marching in columns of ten around the huge building. A Reuther address over a Detroit radio station produced a bonus of favorable publicity when it was learned that the station had censored passages critical of DuPont control of GM and of Alfred P. Sloan, GM's president, as well as lists of profits and executive salaries.

Various corporation maneuvers were countered. GM tried to move work to independent shops, but UAW members there refused to touch "hot dies." The company encouraged back-to-work movements, but there was little scabbing. Since the workers were highly skilled, it was impossible to replace them on short notice. When state police went to Pontiac Fisher Body to provide an escort through the picket lines for returning workers—who failed to materialize—strikers taunted, "Let the state police make . . . tool[s] and dies!"

Homer Martin tried to break the strike. According to a Flint worker, the Martinites imported "paid thugs" to intimidate strikers, necessitating the mobilization and dispatch to trouble spots of the union's "flying squadrons," at times numbering several hundred men. In an attempt to minimize confrontations, Reuther cautioned against provocations and admonished his pickets to "stay sober to avoid unnecessary trouble."

The strike was settled after four weeks. Although GM had "bitterly fought every inch of the way," it accepted the UAW-CIO as exclusive bargaining agent for tool and die makers in forty-two plants. The corporation abandoned its policy of refusing to recognize any union in plants where the CIO and AFL were rivals. In addition, wage rates were standardized and some other improvements in pay and working conditions won. The material gains were not particularly significant; most important was the UAW-CIO's ability to carry the strike through to a successful conclusion, in sharp contrast to the recent efforts of the Martin forces.

Success in the strategy strike provided the momentum to rebuild membership in the UAW-CIO locals and to prepare for federal bargaining-rights elections. Soon after the strike, the National Labor Relations Board conducted elections at Packard, Motor Products, and Briggs that resulted in CIO victories. Eleven of thirteen Chrysler plants voted for UAW-CIO locals with exclusive representation. GM was the next target. Strong campaigns were waged by both CIO and AFL. Lewis, Murray, and Hillman spoke at mass rallies. The Martinites accused the CIO of being under "Red" domination, pointing out, for example, that the tiny American flag imprinted on their opponents' campaign buttons revealingly contained only twenty stars, the number of Soviet republics in the USSR. In the GM election on April 17, 1940, the largest ever held by the NLRB, 128,957 votes—94 percent of those eligible—were cast. The CIO received 84,024, the AFL got 25,911, and 13,919 were voted for neither; the remainder went to other organizations or were invalidated. A new contract brought significant improvements in pay and grievance procedures and established for the first time the important right of the union to challenge the timing of production operations. By mid-1940, the UAW-CIO had contracts with 647 factories and a dues-paying membership of 290,000. Although many had worked for recovery from the blows of the 1937 recession and the Martin split, Reuther received and deserved much of the credit for refounding the union. The victory reconfirmed the UAW's commitment to industrial unionism and paved the way for the organization of all the industry's workers.

The remaining task was the organization of the Ford Motor Company, where earlier campaigns had accomplished little. Ford fired union activists freely and had gotten away with it so far, despite attempts by workers to recover their jobs and back pay through lawsuits and cases before the NLRB.

In 1938, less than a year after the Battle of the Overpass, Reuther again encountered Ford thugs. The occasion was a family birthday party. Expecting a delivery from a Chinese restaurant, he opened the apartment door to two men with drawn revolvers, who forced their way into the room. "Okay, Red," Reuther was told, "you're coming with us." It looked like a one-way ride, and Reuther and his friends fought back. George Edwards warned the gunmen: "You're not getting him out of here. You may shoot some of us, but you won't get out yourselves." Furniture was thrown around, and Reuther wrested a blackjack from one of the attackers. Still no shots had been fired, although Reuther was cut on the face by broken glass. After a friend jumped from a window and went for help, the gangsters left without Reuther. The Detroit police took an hour to arrive, and, once there, did little. A few days later an informer's phone call brought Reuther to a bar packed with union men for protection, where he bought the names of the two gunmen, one a former Ford serviceman. Both were identified in a police lineup by all the guests. The trial was, in Victor's word, a "farce." The defense was allowed to delve into irrelevant political views and the backgrounds of Reuther and the guests, including Reuther's residence in the USSR. On the basis of the unsupported testimony of the gunmen, the defense claimed that Reuther had hired them to fake a kidnapping that would make him a hero to the UAW rank and file. The public prosecutor did not challenge this story or develop the gunmen's connection with Ford. The jury voted for acquittal.

The UAW's final assault on Ford began in the fall of 1940. Workers had won some favorable decisions before the NLRB and the courts. With Martin's AFL threat reduced but not eliminated, the UAW-CIO was stronger than it had been in years. Still, internal rivalries were potentially so disruptive that the CIO sent in a veteran United Mine Workers organizer, Michael Widman, to head the drive. A Dearborn judge held that a local ordinance prohibiting distribution of leaflets in congested areas—meaning the gates of the Ford Motor Company during shift changes—was unconstitutional. The union distributed thousands of copies of a tract called *Ford Facts*, and organizational work began within the plant. Organizers went from door to door in Detroit to locate Ford employees. Within a few months several thousand had joined the UAW, which petitioned the NLRB for representation elections at the Rouge and Lincoln plants. The company, through Harry Bennett, discussed grievances over minor issues with the union.

Suddenly, on April 1, 1941, Bennett precipitated a strike by firing the members of the Rouge grievance committees. Several departments quickly shut down. The UAW leaders, hastening to catch up with their followers, ordered the rest of the work force out of the plant and set up picket lines. Barricades of unionists' cars blocked access. Although many of the black workers joined the strike, several hundred remained inside the plant and launched occasional attacks on the pickets. UAW officials feared a race riot. In 1939 Chrysler had nearly provoked violence by marching almost two hundred black strikebreakers through picket lines under police protection at Dodge Main in Hamtramck, with its largely Polish and antiblack work force. At Ford the UAW mobilized local and national black leaders, including Walter F. White, secretary of the National Association for the Advancement of Colored People (NAACP), to support the strike. Bennett's back-to-work movement collapsed, and many of the blacks inside the plant left. The strike became totally effective.

The new governor of Michigan, Democrat Murray D. Van Wagoner, entered as mediator and ended the strike on April 10, with an agreement to return to the status quo for discharged workers and grievance procedures, and a promise by both sides to hasten an NLRB representation election. With Bennett's encouragement, the AFL offered last-minute competition by chartering a federal union. The UAW-CIO's massive campaign culminated in a rally of more than 60,000 in Detroit's Cadillac Square. The election produced stunning results. At the Rouge, 51,866 workers (70 percent) voted for the UAW-CIO; 20,364 (27 percent) for the AFL; and only 1,958 (3 percent) for no union. Results at other Ford plants were equally decisive. The NLRB certified the UAW-CIO as bargaining agent for Ford workers.

In negotiating its first contract, Ford was on the defensive. Scheduled NLRB hearings on charges of unfair labor practices threatened to reveal a sordid story of company brutality and racketeering. Hoping to head off the investigation, Ford moved ahead quickly with a settlement that gave the UAW far more than it had obtained from anyone else. Ford granted a union shop, requiring all new employees to join the union, and a dues checkoff, important objectives that the UAW had not yet dared to hope for elsewhere. The Ford Service Department was disbanded and plant protection employees required to wear uniforms and badges. In addition, favorable wage, overtime, holiday, seniority, and grievance provisions were won.

One important result of the strike was not in the contract. Over 10,000 black Ford workers joined the UAW, by far the largest entry up to that time. Before the Ford strike there were a few black auto unionists, concentrated in locals at Midland Steel and Bohn Aluminum in Detroit; but only three black organizers were on the union's staff in the late 1930s. After the strike Rouge Local 600—now the largest in the UAW and in the world—had a strong black contingent. Its black officers over the years—Shelton Tappes, Horace Sheffield, Robert Battle III, Marcellius Ivory, and others—played significant roles both in the UAW and in politics. Coming at the outset of the great wartime expansion of production and employment, the creation of a biracial union membership helped to mitigate the destructive force of racial animosity that the war unleashed.

The union's victory was almost more than the elderly Henry Ford could bear. Charles Sorenson, his production chief, later wrote that Ford reacted to the contract with a temper tantrum.

Refusing to sign, he shouted: "I don't want any more of this business. Close the plant down if necessary. Let the union take over if it wishes." Something produced a change of heart, however. By Ford's account, his wife, fearing riots and bloodshed, threatened to leave him unless he accepted the agreement. Reuther thought that Ford had been persuaded the union could be infiltrated, controlled, and perhaps subverted. In any event, the last and most determined opponent of auto unionism had surrendered, ending a decade's campaign for winning the means to a better life.

The establishment of industrial unions in the auto, steel, rubber, and other industries altered United States society and politics. From 1933 to 1941, the unionized proportion of the nonagricultural work force rose from 11.5 to 28.2 percent. During World War II the increase continued, until over one-third of the work force was in unions. Prior to the depression and the New Deal, organized labor had little influence in national affairs. By 1941, however, labor was a major and faithful element in the Roosevelt coalition. Its voice was heard in Congress and the White House. The one-sided concentration of power in the hands of management was gone.

V

Arsenal of Democracy

THE APPROACH OF WORLD WAR II raised new issues for the UAW. The focus of controversy, which raged as furiously as ever, turned from the organization of the workers to national defense and foreign policy. Before Japan plunged the United States into war with the attack on Pearl Harbor on December 7, 1941, differences over preparedness and patriotism agitated all levels of the union.

The UAW's Communist contingent got caught in the squeeze of this momentous shift from domestic to foreign issues, and Reuther quickly moved in to undermine its position in the union. The subservience of the Communists to the USSR was starkly revealed when Hitler and Stalin astounded observers by signing a nonaggression treaty in August 1939, adding a secret provision that divided Poland between them. Within a week Germany launched a blitzkrieg invasion of Poland so rapid and devastating that the Soviets had to move quickly to claim their share. To all but Communist zealots, the Nazi-Soviet pact and the dismemberment of Poland cynically betrayed both principle and the Popular Front position. The proletarian homeland had abetted and profited from aggression in alliance with its ideological opposite. During the two years the pact was in effect, the union's Communists and their remaining friends found that support of the Soviet-Nazi alliance cost them dearly with both the rank and file and the public.

Pressure to curb communist influence in the UAW increased as a result of stepped-up activity by reactionary groups eager to exploit the presence of the Communists for their own purposes. In 1940–1941 the Ku Klux Klan infiltrated several UAW locals whose members it assumed would be receptive to a campaign to force the Communists from the union. Although the degree of their success is uncertain, it was not negligible. Some locals fell under Klan control, and perhaps as many as two hundred delegates to the 1941 UAW convention were Klansmen. If liberal elements like the Reuthers failed to oppose the Communists effectively, control could pass to those who would destroy a democratic, progressive union.

Reuther's first open attack on the UAW Communists and their allies came at the St. Louis convention in August 1940. By then, thanks to German military triumphs and Soviet diplomacy, Hitler controlled central and western Europe; and the USSR had invaded Finland, an act of aggression condemned by Reuther among many others. The St. Louis convention staged a series of strenuous trials of strength, some substantive and some symbolic, between Reuther and the Communists. The votes isolated the Communists, exposed their lack of rank-and-file support, and embarrassed many of their usual allies.

A long, acrimonious debate came on a resolution that condemned "the brutal dictatorships, and wars of aggression of the totalitarian governments of Germany, Italy, Russia and Japan." John Anderson and Nat Ganley of Local 155, the Communists' floor spokesmen, took umbrage at lumping together the Soviet with other totalitarian regimes and complained that the resolution red-baited for the sole purpose of factional advantage. Anderson charged that the Reuthers were turncoats and adduced as proof a partially forged letter written by them from Gorki in which they had expressed enthusiasm for Soviet industrialization. For the other side, one speaker said bluntly that the union must demonstrate that it was not "infested with people who advocate the policies of a foreign government." Both Richard Frankensteen and George Addes supported the resolution, proof that it would have been unpopular and inexpedient to do otherwise; but they tried to minimize the damage to their Communist allies by urging the delegates to stop worrying about international questions and get back on the less treacherous ground of domestic concerns. The union's plain-spoken president, R. J. Thomas, conceded that he must support the resolution in order to be reelected. It carried by a "very large majority," with only about twenty delegates voting against it. Reuther had exposed the delegates' lack of sympathy for the Sovet government and had driven a wedge into the ranks of his opposition.

Another issue, almost as damaging for the Communists, was a resolution to endorse President Roosevelt for reelection. With Roosevelt rendering aid to a Great Britain beleaguered by German air attacks and a threatened invasion, the Nazi-Soviet pact put the Communists in the awkward position of opposing labor's most popular president. In July 1940 Reuther attended as an observer the Democratic national convention that nominated Roosevelt for a third term. Subsequently he secured adoption by the executive board of a resolution proclaiming that "President Roosevelt has been the greatest friend of labor ever to hold the office of President. . . . " John L. Lewis's refusal, for his own reasons, to endorse Roosevelt gave the Communists a pretext to urge defeat of a similar resolution at the convention. Lewis's popularity with auto workers, they hoped, would suffice to defeat it. Wyndham Mortimer attacked the resolution as a "kick in the face" to Lewis, "the greatest labor leader this or any other nation has produced." Nat Ganley accused the president of taking the nation into war. Reuther ridiculed his opponents for hiding behind Lewis's skirts and for their inconsistency. Waving a copy of the minutes of the 1939 convention, he shouted:

> Brother Chairman, I wish I had time to go through this book of proceedings of the last convention, and review the beautiful resolutions that Brother Nat Ganley introduced, praising Roosevelt, because those were the days of collective security and the People's Front. That is no more; there has been a deal between

Stalin and Hitler, and therefore People's Front and collective security have been put in the ash can once and for all.

The cheers for Reuther's speech turned into votes when the endorsement carried by more than 500 to 30. The isolated Communist faction was reduced to its lowest point since the union's founding. In the elections to the executive board, Reuther and his allies gained enough seats to force through a purge of open Communists from the UAW staff. About a half dozen were fired, including Bob Travis, one of the heroes of Flint. The game was being played for keeps.

A few days before the election, Lewis stunned and dismayed labor by endorsing the Republican candidate, Wendell Willkie, and threatening to resign as CIO president if Roosevelt won. The UAW rallied to FDR's support. In a radio broadcast beamed into thirteen industrial cities, Reuther predicted that "the personal spite or the hatred of one man will not switch labor's votes from Mr. Roosevelt. . . . The issue is wholly and simply: Roosevelt or reaction! American labor will take Roosevelt!" And it did. On a tide of votes in labor strongholds, FDR swept to an unprecedented third term.

Soon two controversial strikes rocked the UAW, adding to Communist embarrassment. The first, at the Allis-Chalmers Company in suburban Milwaukee, showed that Reuther would neither oppose the Communists' activities when they were in the union's interest nor support the government uncritically if union issues were at stake. At Allis-Chalmers, Local 248, a militant Communist-dominated local led by Harold Christoffel, squared off against Max D. Babb, the company's union-hating president. The local, charging that the company intended to recognize AFL craft unions among its skilled workmen, struck for a closed shop, one in which only union members could be employed. The strike had been on for seventy-six days when a bloody riot occurred as state troops tried to protect 1,200 men, out of a force of 7,800, who wanted to return to their jobs. The plant closed again, but the strike was finally settled by a government-proposed compromise on a union rather than a closed shop. Allis-Chalmers held about $40 million in contracts for navy turbines. The strike's interruption of defense production pleased Christoffel and Babb, otherwise bitter enemies, since both opposed United States military preparedness. Babb was a supporter of the isolationist America First Committee, who, Reuther suspected, wanted a plant shutdown that he could blame on the UAW.

The Allis-Chalmers strike became a major issue at the 1941 convention in Buffalo when Reuther challenged the credentials of Local 248's delegates, charging that Christoffel disenfranchised workers who refused to follow orders and backed up his rule of the local with a "goon squad"—the "worst kind of strong-arm political racketeering." The convention sent an investigative team to Milwaukee, which reported that Christoffel had vilified the convention delegates as a "bunch of bastards," and the international officers as "nothing but a bunch of phoneys, rats and Hillmanites" for questioning the local's representatives. (*Hillmanite*, meaning a labor official who cooperated with President Roosevelt, was then a term of abuse in the Communist vocabulary.) When new elections were held, the original delegation, including Christoffel, was reelected. Although Reuther took the lead in attacking the leadership's undemocratic methods, he supported the strike, "a glorious battle against one of the most reactionary employers of the country," and refused to attack the local for disrupting defense production.

More serious was the strike at North American Aviation in California in June 1941. With the aircraft industry on the brink of expansion, the UAW launched an organizing campaign, under Frankensteen's direction, with the objects of gaining recognition and raising aircraft industry wages to the standard of the auto workers. Plants of Curtiss-Wright, Douglas, Vought-Sikorsky, and North American were brought under contract. The North American local leadership called a strike while a request for a wage increase was before a government board, violating Frankensteen's pledge that there would be no strike until the board completed its findings. North American produced more than one-fifth of United States military aircraft. Reuther and many others believed that the strike's real aim was to disrupt this production in accord with the political purpose of the Communist party and the USSR. Elmer Freitag, the local's president, had registered as a Communist in a recent election; and Wyndham Mortimer was in charge of West Coast aircraft organizing. Lew Michener, the UAW's California regional director, later acknowledged his Communist party membership at the time of the strike. On June 5 a strike called by the local leadership but unauthorized by the international union shut down the plant after a battle with police. Frankensteen rushed to California to try to end the strike but was shouted-down by hecklers when he spoke. He fired Wyndham Mortimer, ending Mortimer's UAW career. President Roosevelt, who had earlier threatened government action, took the matter out of the union's hands by ordering troops to seize the plant. Production quickly resumed with virtually no opposition, and the workers received a satisfactory retroactive pay settlement.

The North American strike was hotly debated at the Buffalo convention in August 1941. Ironically, since the convention followed the German surprise attack on Russia by several weeks, the Communist line had reversed its direction. From the most extreme isolationists, the Communists overnight became the most fervent anti-Hitler interventionists. Once again, as in 1939, it was clear who pulled the strings. Still there was no question that punishment would be meted out to the disobedient North American local and to Region 6, headed by Michener, for the unauthorized strike. Three proposals came to the floor. The most severe called for Michener's expulsion and placed Region 6 under trusteeship with appointed officers. The most lenient called for barring Michener's reelection to the UAW executive board but leaving him in control of Region 6. The Reuthers supported a middle-of-the-road proposal to suspend Michener from all offices for one year.

All the principals participated in a bitter debate. Michener launched a personal attack on Reuther, claiming that the latter's ambition was to blame for the discord. Although there is no reason to think the delegates accepted this interpretation, they voted by a close margin merely to bar Michener from the executive board, thereby expressing disapproval of the government's use of soldiers to end the strike and responding to an appeal by Frankensteen, eager to mend fences with the left, for clemency.

The most emotional clash at the Buffalo convention came over the so-called Red resolution, a direct attack on Communist power in the international UAW (though not the locals) through a constitutional amendment proposed by Victor Reuther. "No member or supporter," it read, "of any organization whose loyalty [is] to a foreign government or who supports organizations which approve of totalitarian forms of government, shall be eligible to hold elective or appointive office in the International Union or any subdivision thereof." A minority report offered an amendment broadening the exclusion to cover members of communist, Nazi, fascist, and socialist organizations, a transparent device to defeat the resolution by bringing members and friends of the "Royal Family," as their opponents sometimes called the Reuthers, within its scope. After much maneuvering, including an airing of the irrelevant but interesting question of Reuther's draft deferment, a so-called superminority report was adopted by a two-to-one vote, which barred from international UAW offices anyone who "is a member of or subservient to any political organization, such as the Communist, Fascist or Nazi organizations, which owes its allegiance to any government other than the United States or Canada, directly or indirectly." Although this superminority Red resolution went further than Reuther wished, it accorded with his position that those with a loyalty to an outside organization that took precedence over their loyalty to the UAW should be barred from union office. His followers voted for it. Hoping to capitalize on this setback of their opponents, the Reuther caucus ran a candidate for secretary-treasurer against George Addes, who was nevertheless reelected, but by a much reduced margin.

The stakes involved in this ideological and power struggle were manifest in the disorders as well as the debates on the floor. The Buffalo convention was the UAW's most unruly meeting since fights had broken out in Milwaukee in 1937. During the balloting for the executive board, when the minutes reported "considerable confusion in the hall" (a euphemistic phrase for near chaos), President Thomas—who had, as usual, succeeded in staying above the battle—plaintively asked, "What is this, a convention or a riot?" As a result of these elections, however, the nonpolitical unionists, anticommunist Catholics, and independent socialists of the Reuther group for the first time gained a rough parity on the board with their opponents. The entry of the United States into the war postponed, but did not end, the struggle for power in the UAW.

* * *

Months earlier Reuther had turned to the challenging problems of increasing defense production. Following the German victories in western Europe in the summer of 1940, United States public opinion abandoned neutrality in favor of aiding Great Britain and rearming the United States. Although the war potential of American industry was universally acknowledged, the transition to war production was bound to be difficult. Roosevelt established the Office of Production Management (OPM) with General Motors' former chief, William S. Knudsen, in charge, and Sidney Hillman, the CIO troubleshooter, second in command. Many weapons were in short supply, but the most serious shortage was in military aircraft. Reuther advanced a daring and farsighted plan to build "500 Planes a Day," utilizing the car industry's idle capacity. Production of military aircraft in 1940 averaged only twelve planes a day, with an increase to a daily average of sixty-three in 1941.

Aware of the storm the plan would cause, Reuther tried to insure a prompt hearing at the highest levels, first suggesting that R J. Thomas present it directly to President Roosevelt. Thomas, uncertain of its merits and suspicious of Reuther, refused to touch it. "Screw you," he told his colleague, "you're not going to make a horse's ass out of me." Reuther then turned to Philip Murray, head of the steelworkers' union and the CIO's new president, who laid the plan before Roosevelt in December 1940.

Reuther, displaying a talent for nationally publicizing a cause, launched a massive campaign to build public interest and support. The slogan "500 Planes a Day," when the aircraft industry was producing only a handful, grabbed headlines. Thousands of copies of a pamphlet were circulated. Prominent columnists such as Walter Lippmann. Dorothy Thompson, and Ernest K. Lindley reported favorably. President Roosevelt invited Reuther to the White House, where he met with influential New Dealers and cabinet officers, one of whom said, "It probably can be done, but who the hell will pay attention to a squirt of a labor leader?" Henry Morganthau, secretary of the treasury and a Roosevelt confidant, urged the president to order a full study of the plan, but warned: "There is only one thing wrong with the proposal. It comes from the 'wrong' source."

Opposition developed quickly, with aircraft manufacturers aghast. Their spokesmen argued that the precision methods of plane manufacture could not be adapted to mass production. Furthermore, they said, with backing from the Army Air Corps, Reuther's plan would require production of a single model instead of the several types needed. Design modifications suggested by testing and experience would be impossible to implement.

On March 1, 1941, Reuther discussed the plan with OPM head William Knudsen, the key person. They failed to reach agreement, however. Reuther issued a hot statement to the press: "Mr. Knudsen and I met previously, on opposite sides of the table. I thought on this matter of national defense we might sit on the same side. I was mistaken."

One of Reuther's proposals received little attention—his advocacy of an equal role for labor in the management of aircraft production. He suggested creation of an "aviation production board," with "full authority to organize and supervise the mass productions of airplanes," and with representation of labor as well as of government and business. This was the first of several instances in which Reuther put forward labor's claim to share in management authority, a reformulation of socialist principles adapted to and built on the successful establishment of industrial unions. These unions could become the instruments for collective decision making in industry. Company spokesmen were strongly opposed; other labor leaders, with the exception of Murray, showed little interest. Both within and outside the UAW, most of labor believed that capitalism needed no modifications beyond recognition of unions as their members' agents.

The immediate question was whether auto industry machine tools could be converted to aircraft manufacture. Knudsen doubted that they could, although, once Pearl Harbor forced abandonment of "business as usual," he told a news conference that "conversion [to military production] is tool-making. Take all these machines you have and see if there isn't some way to utilize them." Two years later K. T. Keller, president of the Chrysler Corporation, testified before a Senate committee that 89 percent of Chrysler's machine tools had been converted to war production. The publisher Philip Graham, interpreting the statement in the way most favorable to his friend, said that this meant Reuther had been 89 percent correct. After the war *Fortune* magazine remarked that "Reuther was on the right track."

Although the plan was rejected, it brought its author national attention and put him in touch with influential Washington figures, including both the president and Mrs. Eleanor Roosevelt. The war effort needed men with ideas and a talent for dramatizing proposals. Sometimes, however, Reuther's ideas were too dramatic, if not quixotic. He suggested, for example, kicking off a national scrap metal drive by dismantling the iron fence around the White House. Shortly after Pearl Harbor he proposed a condensed period of military training for American workers to resist an enemy invasion. Later in the war he devised a "portable foxhole," an updated suit of armor for the modern soldier. Several technical projects proved of value, however. The aircraft industry used ground gears in engines, which required a long and costly manufacturing process. Reuther suggested that the cheaper and more quickly produced shaved gears, like those used in cars, would work as well. Although the Air Corps was hard to convince, Reuther did so, and engine production increased. Another idea broke a bottleneck in the manufacture of 75 millimeter guns for the tanks that were being built faster than they could be armed. The traditional method of honing a gun barrel required ten hours. Reuther, with the help of UAW machinists, proposed that the barrels be broached by drawing them through a series of rings of sawlike teeth to obtain the exact size. Broaching took only about one minute.

Reuther was a member of several wartime boards and committees, such as the Labor-Management Policy Committee of the War Manpower Commission, charged with coordinating the supply of available workers with production needs. He was called in for advice by Sidney Hillman of OPM; Robert P. Patterson, undersecretary of war; Harold C. Ickes, secretary of the interior; Mrs. Eleanor Roosevelt; and even the president himself. On one occasion President Roosevelt greeted Reuther at a White House meeting with a warm handshake and the gracious compliment, "Here's my young red-headed engineer!" which provoked R. J. Thomas to blurt out: "He's not an engineer! He's just a tool and die maker!"

Reuther was asked by both Ferdinand Eberstadt, the materials chief of the War Production Board and author of the successful strategic materials allocation system, and Charles E. Wilson, former president of General Electric and then a high War Production Board official, to serve as their deputy; but he declined. Roosevelt considered having Reuther head a new agency for war production planning or, alternatively, giving him an army commission with duty as a presidential aide on production. Both proposals ran into opposition from labor magnates, with AFL president William Green exclaiming, "Why, Reuther's just a kid!" Another version held that Reuther's FBI

unions. The unions could still discuss grievances, but the no-strike pledge limited their power to resolve them. Beyond that, there was little for them to do. Their claim on the workers' support and loyalty was correspondingly reduced. The friendly Roosevelt administration, however, had no intention of undermining unions in the midst of a war requiring national unity. It needed the support of union leaders to make labor mobilization policies work. To provide union security, the government included a "maintenance of membership" formula in its contracts. In effect, this established a modified union shop in which workers in a unionized plant, unless they withdrew from the union within fifteen days after beginning work, had to remain in the union for the term of the contract. Less than 1 percent withdrew. Total union membership expanded from 10.5 million in December 1941 to 14.75 million by June 1945, essentially completing organization of the nation's basic industries.

For the first year of the war, the UAW was at peace with itself. Prewar factionalism subsided in the face of patriotism and the American military alliance with the USSR. Early in 1943 the Communists abruptly disrupted this harmony when Earl Browder, the party's chairman, demanded that wages be converted to piece rates, or incentive pay, to increase production. Piece rates, widely employed in Russian industry, had once been common in auto parts manufacture but were hated by workers. Consequently, the union had won their replacement with hourly wages. The proposal was bound to be unpopular, but the Communists in the UAW and those Noncommunist leaders who relied on them followed the line. George Addes proposed an incentive-pay plan at an executive board meeting, and Richard Frankensteen argued that the total wages of aircraft workers would increase if the plan won approval. Reuther attacked the proposal, and the majority of the board sided with him. His position was overwhelmingly confirmed at the 1943 convention.

The fight over incentive pay reopened the factional struggle. In 1943 the Reuther caucus ran a candidate against Addes for secretary-treasurer in a lively campaign stressing the subservience of Addes and Frankensteen to Moscow. To the tune of "Reuben and Rachel," Reuther backers sang:

> Who are the boys who take their orders
> Straight from the office of Joe Sta-leen?
> No one else but the gruesome twosome,
> George F. Addes and Frankensteen.
> Who are the boys that fight for piecework,
> To make the worker a machine?
> No one else but the gruesome twosome,
> George F. Addes and Frankensteen. . . .
>
> The Auto Workers have their sideshow.
> One is fat and one is lean.
> Who are they but the gruesome twosome,
> George F. Addes and Frankensteen.

The Addes forces replied with verses of their own, but the Reutherites had the better song. Addes won reelection by a slim margin over his opponent; but Reuther was chosen first vice-president over Frankensteen by a mere 345 votes, the only time he bested Frankensteen in a direct challenge. On the executive board the Reuther group expanded to nearly equal Addes's following, with President Thomas controlling a few votes in the middle. The incentive-pay issue, by demonstrating Communist willingness to sacrifice a significant gain and his rivals' dependence on their support, bolstered Reuther's standing.

The auto industry changed dramatically during the war years. No cars for civilian use were produced from 1942 until 1945, but production of military equipment more than took up the slack. The industry manufactured about one-fifth of the nation's entire military output, including, in addition to tanks and trucks, 87 percent of the aircraft bombs, 85 percent of the steel helmets, 75 percent of the aircraft engines, over 12 billion rounds of small arms ammunition, and a host of other products. The industry showed that it possessed the greatest concentration of large-scale metal-fabricating machinery and knowledge in the world, contributing as much as anyone or anything to Allied victory.

The work force and the UAW were equally transformed. The numbers employed and union membership mounted rapidly. By the end of the war UAW membership was over 1.2 million, of whom about 350,000 were women, making it the largest free union in the world, with a female membership matched only by one other union, the United Electrical Workers. Although wage rates were controlled, steady work and plenty of overtime boosted incomes. With additional family members recruited for the work force, household income and savings rose to record levels. The Detroit area attracted more than 230,000 new residents, including 80,000 blacks, between 1940 and 1945.

Production records and riches were not the whole story, however. As *Life* said, "Detroit is Dynamite"; it "can either blow up Hitler or it can blow up the U.S." The influx of newcomers produced intense competition for housing and services. Many of the new residents were southerners, both black and white. A series of racial incidents occurred at public housing sites and elsewhere, bringing the city to the brink of a racial explosion. In June 1943 the most destructive race riot of the war broke out in Detroit. Two days of savage street warfare resulted in the deaths of twenty-five blacks and nine whites and property damage of more than $2 million. The mayor estimated that 100,000 white rioters took part, and federal troops were called in to restore order. The auto plants were free of violence during the riot, however, and UAW officials proudly pointed out that blacks and whites continued to work side by side. Reuther, in later testimony before a Senate committee, claimed that the UAW "had created an oasis of sanity in a city gone mad with frustration, bitterness, bigotry, and brutality." However, the fact that three-quarters of the black workers and half of the whites were absent from work during the riot suggests that workers were either involved or afraid to come to the plants.

Although the riot was kept out of the plants, racial strife of lesser magnitude frequently occurred. Trouble began even before the United States entered the war with "hate strikes," which could be either wildcat walkouts or brief sit-downs by

whites in plants where blacks were being transferred or up-
graded to better jobs as defense contracts expanded employment and production. After December 1941 the no-strike
pledge bound the officers of the UAW; but elements of the rank
and file, abetted at times by local officers, sometimes took
matters into their own hands.

The worst situation developed at Packard, located on Detroit's
East Side, with large numbers of southern-born and Polish-
American workers, and a management that at times was openly
racist. The company's personnel officer, for example, during a
dispute over the transfer of two black metal polishers from auto
to defense work, insisted that metal polishing was "a white man's
job." Packard Local 190 had been a Ku Klux Klan target.
Perhaps as many as half of its delegates to the 1941 convention
were Klansmen, and Klan agitation continued at the plant
during the war. The climax of months of racial incidents came in
June 1943, only a few weeks before the riot, when 25,000
Packard workers walked out over the upgrading of three blacks
to assembly line work. Quick responses from R. J. Thomas, who
threatened to expel those union members participating in the
strike, and, more important, from the Army Air Corps' Detroit
representative, who said he would fire them, ended the wildcat
in three days, but not before nearly thirty ringleaders were
suspended. Ultimately several lost their jobs. Over the next few
months negotiations among union, management, and government representatives resulted in promotions for significant
numbers of black workers.

The gap between commitments of the leadership and the
inclinations of elements in the rank and file was greater on racial
issues than on anything else. The international leadership supported the union's constitutional requirement of nondiscrim-
inatory treatment and its moral commitment to equality and
workers' solidarity. Certain locals, particularly the giant Rouge
Local 600, with many black members and black officers, kept the
pressure on the international to honor these pledges. Furthermore, the union's Communists were strong, vocal champions of

black rights. Reuther warned the hate strikers that the UAW would not defend their jobs. In April 1943, in the midst of the conflict, he was the only UAW international officer to appear at a Cadillac Square rally against racial discrimination. "The UAW-CIO," he said, "would tell any worker that refused to work with a colored worker that he could leave the plant because he did not belong there."

Reuther objected to a proposal to create a black seat on the executive board, even though black membership rose to approximately 100,000 during the war. At the 1943 convention nearly all of the black delegates—at 8 percent of the total the largest representation to that time—united in its support. Most were allied with the Addes faction, and Reuther's opposition probably stemmed in part from a fear of diluting his support on the narrowly divided board. However, at the convention the Reuther forces attacked the proposal on principle as a Jim Crow device. Victor Reuther declared that "if there is a special post for Negroes, then in all justice there should be a post at large for the Catholics, the women, the Jews, the Poles, and all the rest." Walter predicted that the proposal would foster delay and irresponsibility in confronting the union's racial problems. Oversimplifying the situation and the solution, he said, "the problem does not exist in the executive board,—the problem exists in the shops, and that is where it has to be licked." The resolution failed.

Both Addes's and Reuther's caucuses supported creation of a minorities department to focus the union's attack on discrimination and racism within its ranks. At the 1944 convention a Fair Practices Commission was established, headed by George W. Crockett, a black and an Addes supporter. In 1946 a Fair Practices and Anti-Discrimination Department was set up; following the shift of power within the union, William Oliver, a black from Ford Local 400 and a Reuther supporter, was placed in charge. Both Crockett and Oliver conducted educational projects and worked out solutions to racial problems within the guidelines of the union's constitution.

In sum, the UAW's record in difficult wartime circumstances was constructive. Employment of blacks crossed a watershed in the war years. Even without a seat on the executive board, their voice became much stronger within the union, and they repeatedly won the leadership's support.

As the war's end approached, government restrictions, corporate profiteering, and deteriorating conditions in the plants provoked mounting opposition to the no-strike pledge. To many workers, the union leadership seemed more interested in holding the work force in line behind the war effort than in advancing their interests. Wage rate controls, which held wages below price increases and sharply contrasted with the absence of effective controls on salaries, were only one issue undermining allegiance to the no-strike pledge. Even when pay raises were justified under government regulations, slow processing and approval by the War Labor Board provoked rebellious feelings. Delays in settling grievances had become chronic. With the threat of a strike removed, settlements of even routine disagreements over contract interpretation and compliance were stalled or ignored. Whether delay was deliberate on the companies' part or the result of an overloaded wartime bureaucracy (since grievances ultimately were referred to a government agency), the result was frustrating to those who worked under adverse conditions.

Disputes over piece rates and production standards, hours of work, health and safety concerns, transfers and promotions, and a host of other issues sparked a succession of short-lived but widespread wildcat strikes in 1943 and 1944. In the spring of 1944, for example, wildcats involving several thousand workers in each instance occurred at Chevrolet Gear and Axle, Ford Highland Park, Ford Rouge, and Chrysler Highland Park—all in the Detroit area. Similar actions broke out elsewhere. Worker militancy was encouraged by the labor shortage. If you were fired for wildcatting from one shop, it was easy to get another job.

When the 1944 convention met in Grand Rapids, a newly

formed rank-and-file caucus, which drew heavily on Reuther locals, forced debate on the no-strike pledge. The Addes-Frankensteen caucus supported the pledge without reservation, as their Communist allies, who would brook no interruptions of production damaging to the USSR, insisted. "The party line," one observer wrote, "is taking a suicidal turn in favor of the Chamber of Commerce—and such positions do not sit well with the rank-and-file." The ill-fitting patriot's mantle donned for the occasion by the tribunes of the left excited the ridicule of their opponents. As Addes defended the pledge and invoked the necessity of wartime sacrifice in a convention speech, the delegates from the militant but independent and noncommunist Briggs Local 212, who opposed its continuation, vigorously waved tiny American flags in mockery.

Reuther, to his detriment, advanced a compromise on the pledge, proposing to maintain it in plants producing war material but not in those manufacturing civilian goods after the Allies had won the war against Germany. Critics charged that companies would retain a little war work to avoid strikes while shifting most of their production to civilian articles. Although refinements of the proposal to meet this objection were not difficult to formulate, it went down on an unrecorded vote, a sharp rebuke to Reuther for his attempted straddle of the issue. Earlier the convention had rejected the rank-and-file caucus's proposed repeal of the pledge by nearly a two-to-one margin; it next narrowly voted down adherence to the pledge. All three proposals were defeated. An alert rank-and-file leader asked if this triple play meant the UAW had no policy on wartime strikes, a silence that would leave each local free to set its course. The embarrassed leadership quickly proposed to submit the pledge to an extraordinary membership mail ratification vote, which eventually upheld it by a substantial margin.

The prospect of peace stimulated Reuther's thinking. Again he drew on his socialist heritage for guidance, emphasizing cooperation, public coordination, and a broad distribution of income and goods. Although many feared a depression, he was optimistic. He saw national planning in which all elements—labor as well as business and government—were represented as the key to a prosperous, secure future. In 1944 he proposed a sixteen-point conversion program that included pooling manpower and machine tools for allocation among corporations, a thirty-hour work week to guarantee employment for all, government operation of monopolistic industries as yardsticks for determining costs, and the establishment of production quotas based on social need. Later Reuther urged creation of a Peace Production Board with representatives of labor, management, consumers, agriculture, and government to allocate manpower, materials, and machinery.

The huge government investment in plants and machinery should be put to peacetime uses as soon as the war ended, Reuther thought. The most pressing need, he believed, was for mass-produced, prefabricated, low-cost housing. Government-owned aircraft factories could readily be converted to this purpose. Venturing into more hazardous depths for an auto workers' union leader, he proposed that huge government-owned plants in the Detroit area, such as the Willow Run bomber plant and the Chrysler Tank Arsenal, be converted to the manufacture of "modern streamlined light-metal railroad cars." The *Detroit News*, appalled that an upstart union official should discuss such a weighty matter, sarcastically urged the UAW to buy Willow Run to "manufacture . . . whatever it thinks may strike the fancy of the market. . . . The experiment would be edifying . . . as a yardstick both on the performance of managements and, even more so, on the union leaders' confident ideas of how management ought to perform." For the car manufacturer's consideration, Reuther suggested a sliding scale of variable prices. The laudable aim was to moderate the irregular employment that resulted from seasonal swings in auto production. As the slow season approached, prices would be reduced; during peak seasons they would be increased. Management, anticipating a booming postwar market, made no public comment.

With the normal processes of collective bargaining suspended in wartime, Reuther discovered new forums of leadership. Seizing opportunities, he showed that he could operate as confidently in the national milieu as at union headquarters or on the picket line. He established a reputation as an imaginative thinker who could effectively represent labor to government offices, testify before Congress, and joust with the national press. These skills were essential for effective leadership of the UAW, with its wide range of political and social as well as economic goals.

Illustrations

Photographs reprinted by permission of The Archives of Labor and Urban Affairs, Wayne State University.

Tool and die shop of the Wheeling Steel Company, Wheeling, West Virginia, c. 1927, where Walter Reuther learned his trade. Reuther is at the upper right wearing the cap.

Walter Reuther (seated, center) and Victor Reuther (standing, far right) with fellow tool room workers in the Gorki automobile factory, 1934.

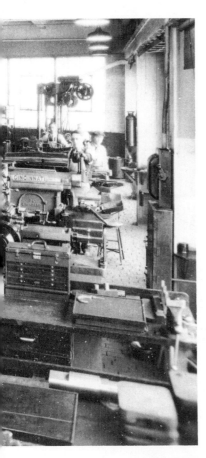

Union officers and auto workers march out of the Cadillac plant in Detroit on January 17, 1937, after the sit-down strike. Left to right: Julius Hochman, Richard Frankensteen, Leo Krzycki, Homer Martin, and Walter Reuther.

Walter Reuther, Richard Frankensteen (second from right), and two other UAW organizers on the overpass as Ford Motor Company Service Department employees approach, May 26, 1937.

Reuther and Frankensteen after the beatings, May 26, 1937.

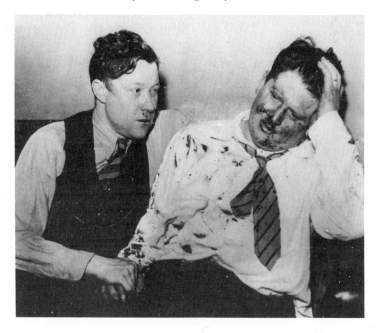

Roy, Victor, and Walter Reuther (left to right) at the UAW's 1937 convention, Milwaukee.

Walter Reuther explains strategy to striking GM tool-and-die makers, 1939. Victor Reuther is seated on the left.

Reuther and supporters celebrate his election as UAW president, 1946. Roy Reuther is second from the left.

UAW members particpate in the Washington, D.C., civil rights demonstration and march, August 1963.

Reuther, Martin Luther King, Jr. (center left), and Whitney Young (center) on the steps of the Lincoln Memorial, Washington, D.C., during the civil rights demonstration, 1963.

Reuther addresses the UAW's 1970 convention.

VI

Victory Out of Defeat

THE WAR'S END brought new perils for workers. Conversion to peacetime production went slowly, with even longer delays threatening. Although a new depression did not materialize, labor market dislocations were painful. More than 300,000 Michigan war workers lost their jobs after V-J Day, and entire industries faced shutdown. For organized labor, the historical precedents were ominous. After World War I an aggressive open shop campaign had reduced a growing labor movement to impotence for a decade. Reuther warned that if the UAW's determination wavered, "it would be 1919 and the twenties all over again."

The political future also seemed stormy. On April 12, 1945, Franklin D. Roosevelt died. Although Harry S. Truman, the new president, had supported the New Deal and labor as a senator, to nearly everyone, friend and foe alike, he seemed a lesser man than his predecessor. Labor's influence in Congress continued to decline. Since 1938 a coalition of Republicans and conservative Democrats had grown in power, and all signs pointed to a continuation of the trend. The results of the congressional elections of 1946 and the passage of the probusiness Taft-Hartley Act the following year confirmed labor's fears. On the other hand, the democratic left in western Europe gained power after the war. The victory of the union-backed British Labour party in the July 1945 elections, foreshadowing the creation of a workers' welfare state, was especially heartening to Reuther. If labor acted boldly, holding out the promise of a better future for all, it might avert reaction and fashion a social democratic society.

The unstable equilibrium of forces within the UAW was poised for movement. The standing of all the UAW's leaders, regardless of faction, had been damaged by growing discontent in the ranks towards the war's end. The time was ripe to seize the initiative, vent the pent-up grievances of wartime, and direct the workers' energy and commitment toward a constructive end. All the UAW's prominent figures, including Addes, Thomas, Frankensteen, and Leonard, had now drawn together in a shaky, defensive combination against Reuther. The struggle over the UAW's future direction and over who would lead it was about to be renewed.

Management, too, was spoiling for a fight. As *New York Times* columnist James Reston remarked of the auto industry, "both sides seem to take the view that they have taken a lot of guff from the other side during the war and are now free to fight it out." This condition was general. From the summer of 1945 through the end of 1946, there were more strikes with more participants than in any similar period before or since, with disputes in the auto, steel, electrical equipment, meat-packing, longshoring, and trucking industries.

The longest and most bitterly contested strike was that of the General Motors workers, which began in November 1945 and lasted 113 days. In prestrike negotiations, Reuther advanced a novel and controversial objective, demanding, in addition to a 30 percent wage increase, a pledge from GM to hold the line on car prices. In the past, he said, the auto companies had in effect conducted two sets of negotiations. On one side, they negotiated wages and working conditions over the bargaining table with their employees. On the other, they negotiated car prices in the marketplace with consumers. Reuther proposed that the union participate in both sets of decisions. Its participation was necessary, he argued, because of the risk of inflation if management alone set prices and because consumers could not bargain effectively in a market dominated by a few giant firms. The 30 percent wage increase would maintain but not exceed the auto workers' overtime-swollen wartime incomes. The price pledge would block an inflationary surge that could lead to unemployment and depression, while allowing the company to give stockholders a fair return and to accumulate investment capital.

Reuther believed that mass purchasing power, broadly distributed among all workers, was the key to future prosperity, but that neither government nor business nor consumers alone could create and sustain it. Only unions, transcending their customary role and responsibility, could discipline the corporations on prices and prevent their members' wages from being paid in "the wooden nickels of inflation." "All that we have done in this wage case," Reuther asserted, "is say that we are not going to operate as a narrow economic pressure group which says 'we are going to get ours and the public be damned' or 'the consumer be damned.' We say that we want to make progress with the community and not at the expense of the community." More than any other labor leader of his time, Reuther placed the unions in the vanguard of a broad social advance for all.

Reuther's proposal angered management and upset some union leaders. GM charged that it undermined management prerogatives and was socialistic. In discussions before the strike, Reuther and Harry Coen, a corporation executive, exchanged blows:

Reuther: "Unless we get a more realistic distribution of America's wealth, we don't get enough to keep this machinery going."

Coen: "There it is again. You can't talk about this thing without exposing your socialistic desires."

Reuther: "If fighting for equal and equitable distribution of the wealth of this country is socialistic, I stand guilty of being a Socialist."

Coen: "I think you are convicted."

Reuther: "I plead guilty."

The corporation resisted, determined to restrict the UAW's role to the concerns with wages and working conditions characteristic of "business unionism." Rejecting the union's "unreasonable demands," it countered with an offer to increase the work week to forty-four hours with no payment of premium rates, thereby raising the incomes of those with jobs. As Reuther pointed out, GM's proposal would almost certainly increase unemployment.

Both sides maneuvered for advantage and elaborated on their proposals in the sparring that preceded the strike. Reuther offered to accept less than 30 percent if GM proved it could not make a fair profit. However, the corporation would have to let the union have "a look at the books," opening its entire cost and earnings records to union inspection. The corporation again charged encroachment on management prerogatives, with one of its officials candidly confessing, "We don't even let our stockholders look at the books." A union victory on this point, the corporation added, would lead to "a Socialistic nation with all activities controlled and regimented, and with the people the servants of government."

Reuther miscalculated in counting on GM's eagerness to enter the vast postwar sellers' car market to produce an acceptable agreement. Largely because of the tax laws, GM could afford to be stubborn. Under the wartime excess profits tax, which was still in effect, GM's loss of revenues from a strike could be subtracted from its federal tax bill. The corporation had already earned nearly as much for 1945 as it was allowed before losing all additional profit to the tax. Since the taxes had been paid on the basis of uninterrupted production, it would receive rebates if forced to close down. In effect, the government would make strike payments to the corporation. According to *Business Week*, the strike cost GM only 15 cents for each dollar reduction in its earnings. As the magazine wrote, "Never before, perhaps, has a major employer had so little direct economic incentive to end a stoppage by making concessions to a union." Although GM did not want to lose sales to competitors and risk permanent loss of a portion of its clientele, the direct cost of the strike was low. From that perspective, a worse time for a strike could hardly be imagined.

A strike authorization vote, however, expressed the ordinary worker's sentiments and strengthened Reuther's hand. The wartime Smith-Connally Act, still in effect, required that the question presented to the workers be worded thus: "Do you wish to permit an interruption of war production in wartime as a result of this dispute?" Since the war had been over for two months when the vote was held, no one was fooled. The authorization carried by nearly a six-to-one margin. At the last moment the corporation offered a 10 percent raise, which Reuther countered with an arbitration proposal framed in such a way that GM would have to concede public examination of its books. On November 21 the strike of 320,000 GM workers began.

Although the strike challenged the status quo, provoked heated exchanges, and lasted much longer than any previous auto strike, it was peaceful. The corporation made no effort to operate. Symbolic picket lines were set up for the sake of publicity and morale, but there was no need to block access to the plants.

Reuther recruited a citizens' committee of sympathetic prominent persons to investigate his claim that GM could afford higher wages without a price increase. To no one's surprise, its report supported his position and warmly praised his effort to lift bargaining "to a new high level by insisting that the advancement of labor's interest shall not be made at the expense of the public." Within the UAW and the labor movement, however, Reuther encountered skepticism and hostility. No important labor leader, left-wing or otherwise, supported his contention that unions bore a responsibility for the general welfare as well as that of their members. CIO President Philip Murray endorsed the strike but privately tried to talk Reuther out of his concern with prices. UAW president R. J. Thomas spoke a few words in its behalf but ridiculed Reuther's proposals as offering food for thought for intellectuals but little bread for workers. As usual, John L. Lewis's criticism was harsh. In testimony before the House Labor Committee, he contemptuously dismissed the "poor blundering leaders of the United Automobile Workers [for choosing] this time of all times to shut down General Motors." "The dishonesty" of the company, he added, was "only equalled by the stupidity on the side of the labor organization."

In early December, President Truman intervened by appointing a fact-finding board. The corporation, fearing that the board would link a wage increase with prices and demand access to the company's records, offered a raise of 13½ cents. On December 20 the fact-finding board met with GM representatives. A fresh statement from President Truman was read, which said that the board "should have the authority ... to examine the books of the employer," whereupon GM walked out of the hearings and denounced the attempt to force it to open its books to "the hungry eyes of ... competitors." The company must, a spokesman said, defend itself against the "revolutionary" and "radical" position of the union and the government. "To yield," he added, "would mean the end of ... free enterprise."

On January 10, 1946, the board recommended a raise of 17.5 percent, 19½ cents an hour, which, as far as it could determine, the corporation could afford without a price increase. Reuther, though privately disappointed in these terms, which were little more than half the original demand, announced that he would accept on condition that the corporation agreed. GM quickly turned the proposal down.

With the strike now nearly three months old, Reuther had to rally GM workers and the public. A strikers' relief committee raised a large sum, which was badly needed since the union had no strike fund. Union speakers descended on civic clubs and other local organizations to present the workers' side. Letters were sent to businessmen in cities with GM facilities, pointedly asking how many members of the DuPont family, the corporation's largest stockholders, they had among their customers, compared with the number of GM workers. To show solidarity, Reuther donated his pay to strikers' relief.

He tried to force President Truman to take action by sending him a well-publicized telegram in which he argued, with merit, that the union was upholding the administration's price-stabilization program. "The fight of the General Motors workers is your fight and the fight of every American. It demands your immediate and militant support." The president, however, resenting the pressure and preoccupied with other disputes, was persuaded by his secretary of labor that Reuther had mismanaged the strike and was trying to enlist Truman in the cause in order to save a faltering bid for the UAW presidency. Truman refused to do anything and thereby, not for the last time, failed to support the recommendation of the board he had appointed.

Reuther's effort was undermined by settlements reached with other employers. Ford and Chrysler, who originally had offered their workers no pay raise at all, agreed with the UAW on hourly wage increases of 18 cents and 18½ cents, respectively, with a stipulation that the contracts could be reopened if GM agreed to pay more. Nothing was said about prices. The most damaging settlement, at 18½ cents without a pledge on prices, was that of the United Electrical Workers (UE), who represented 30,000 GM employees in electrical equipment divisions. UAW officials charged that UE had reneged on a promise not to negotiate a separate settlement without prior consultation. Many, including Reuther, saw a clear explanation for this betrayal. UE's leaders were close to the Communist party, and Reuther believed the agreement was a deliberate attempt to discredit him at the expense of GM workers. The UAW's position was further weakened when the United Steel Workers settled for the now customary 18½ cents, with the steel companies promised a $5 a ton price increase by the government. Truman undercut his program of price stability in order to end that strike, with the concurrence of Philip Murray, president of the steelworkers' union as well as of the CIO. As Reuther later said, "The torch we lit during the General Motors strike was not picked up by the Steelworkers." A few days later the rubber workers agreed to the same terms, and the pattern for the first postwar round of wage settlements and inflationary price increases was set.

By the end of February only one cent an hour separated the two sides. Many GM workers, their savings exhausted, were ready to quit. As a blunt Cadillac welder wrote R. J. Thomas, "For God's sake, shut up Walter Reuther and get us back to work. . . . Most of my savings are gone—and all of my patience— and there are a lot more in the same shape. For real gains, the strike is lost. . . . The quicker we cut the loss until another try, the better."

On March 13, 1946, agreement to end the strike was reached at a meeting between Murray and President Charles E. Wilson of GM, with no UAW official present. The company agreed to an 18½ cent raise, with adjustments for plant pay differentials, vacations, and overtime that the union claimed raised the total to slightly more than 19½ cents. In addition, the union gained a dues checkoff and stronger contractual seniority clauses, but the agreement was silent on prices.

Reuther's proclamation of victory rang hollow. Workers elsewhere had done nearly as well with shorter strikes or even none at all. It would be more than two years before the GM workers recovered their pay losses, and not until 1953 would their earnings equal what they would have made from GM's earlier offer of 13½ cents. The direct cost of the strike to industry and labor was more than $1 billion.

An ascending spiral of price and wage increases ensued, with government no more successful than the union in restraining prices. Within six months the car companies were granted three price increases. Then Congress, abolishing all price controls, took off the lid. Prices and profits roared upward, with the cost-of-living index rising at a faster pace in 1947 than in any subsequent year until 1979. By 1949, when the car companies had completed the transition to peacetime production, they had an annual rate of return (net profits after taxes divided by net worth) of over 25 percent, compared with less than 9 percent for all corporations.

The GM strike was Reuther's boldest attempt to transcend the destructive competition of interest groups and create a partnership for the common good. The experiment failed because neither government nor business—nor even most of labor's leadership and rank and file—had the vision or the will to transcend traditional roles. The strike demonstrated the limits of the union's power to create a new distribution of social and economic responsibilities. Although he never surrendered his belief in a community role for labor, Reuther realistically realigned his objectives for both the union and politics in general toward less sweeping change.

Although the strike failed, it propelled Reuther into the UAW's presidency, a result he doubtless intended. The UAW's militant challenge to GM and Reuther's aggressive leadership pleased many workers. Since the strike's failure had resulted in part from the inconstancy of other labor leaders, Reuther appeared dedicated to—even a martyr for—the worker's cause. Never lacking in self-confidence, ambition, or ability, he was the kind of man who took for granted that anyone who agreed with his views would be a follower. At the appropriate time he was sure to challenge R. J. Thomas, whom he had never considered qualified for the presidency.

Reuther lacked the common touch that Thomas amply possessed, but he more than compensated in other ways. After union meetings Reuther went home instead of joining in the "barroom postmortems" where "the boys hash it all over." Not all auto workers, however, and especially not the crucial second echelon of leaders in locals and on the UAW staff, were genial hail fellows in the Thomas mold. Reuther combined a formidable list of qualities, abilities, and practical skills. In 1946 he was thirty-eight and looked younger. His hard work, self-discipline, oratorical creativity, and leadership talents—along with his independent, anticommunist left-of-center position—

added up to what many thought the UAW needed in a president. His "Boy Scout simplicity and enthusiasm," wrote a friendly journalist, "shines through everything he does. All of his enterprises," the writer continued, "are tackled with a happy, bustling vigor that breeds confidence in those associated with him."

Reuther knew his presidential bid would be opposed by CIO president Philip Murray. Earlier such opposition would have been fatal, but by 1946 the UAW was sufficiently strong and independent to ignore CIO wishes. Reuther and Murray had cooperated on many projects, but there was always a suspicious wariness between them. Murray, then trying to hold together the CIO's shaky alliance of incompatible elements, uneasily eyed the ambitious, impatient younger man. President Truman once told Murray, following a meeting at which Reuther was present, "Phil, that young man is after your job." "No, Mr. President," Murray replied, "he really is after your job."

The "Reuther boom" began early in March, when presidents of seventeen locals, representing an impressive combined membership of 250,000, announced their support. The surest and least divisive route to the presidency was to neutralize George Addes, who was informed that he could continue as secretary-treasurer in a Reuther administration. Addes, known to be unhappy with Thomas, was tempted but finally decided against a deal. Playing second fiddle to Reuther held no attraction, and he was reluctant to abandon old allies.

At the convention in Atlantic City, feeling spilled over in heckling and rowdiness in the caucuses, hotel lobbies, and bars. At one point Addes, a humorless man, unintentionally brought down the house with a plea to the members to stop dropping paper bag water bombs from hotel windows because they might injure "a delegate or a human being." Murray, who could not afford to antagonize the UAW's next president—whoever he might be—concluded a speech with an oblique but unmistakable endorsement of Thomas, "this great big guy for whom I have a distinct fondness, the President of your Union." The Reuther forces counterattacked with a proposal for an off-the-record debate between the two candidates at a closed session. They were confident that the quick-thinking, fast-talking, nimble Reuther would demolish his opponent. Addes, temporarily chairing the convention, blocked the debate by ruling that two-thirds approval was required for such a session, a vote the Reuther forces could not muster. They gained a majority, however, so this early test of strength cast a chill over the Thomas-Addes coalition.

The election was contested in delegates' meetings and caucuses. In hard-hitting speeches, Reuther attacked the Thomas-Addes leadership's alliance with the Communist faction, which had forced them to accept a Soviet-dictated party line often in conflict with the needs of the union. He cited their wartime support of incentive pay, a categorical no-strike pledge, and labor mobilization, and assailed UE's recent sell-out in the GM strike. Nor did he fail to point out that the antiunion, anti-Soviet reaction, as United States–Soviet relations turned hostile at the beginning of the Cold War, "makes this union vulnerable, at a high time when we should be putting on armored plates." The conspicuous presence in the UAW of champions of Soviet positions on international political issues gave labor's enemies their most effective weapon for an all-out assault on unions.

Three major elements, along with other scattered supporters, united in the Reuther, or right-wing, caucus to form a majority. The largest and most important were nonideological unionists whose patience with the endless factional quarrels had run out. Many Reuther delegates were attending their first convention. They and their constituents revolted against the far left and its allies, whom they blamed for internal dissension. As antilabor forces stepped up their attack on unions, a fragmented leadership, regardless of ideological orientations, became a costly extravagance the UAW could no longer afford. Reuther also had substantial support from the Association of Catholic Trade Unionists (ACTU), an expression of Catholic social conscience and the spearhead of the union's anticommunist forces. The alliance of the secular Reuther with the ACTU was based on more than expediency and anticommunism, however. A kinship existed between their concepts of industrial justice, expressed in common advocacy of a role for labor in governing the workplace, in joint labor-management planning, and in support for even so specific a proposal as a guaranteed annual wage. Given the large number of Catholics in the UAW, the ACTU was a powerful force. The socialists in the Reuther camp, though fewer in number, were politically sophisticated veterans of many battles, capable debaters, and experienced organizers.

Both sides made ample use of the standard political devices of promises to waverers, offers of jobs, and arm-twisting. Personal attacks, such as Reuther's characterization of Thomas as a "desperate man . . . doing his best to hang onto a swivel chair," and the Thomas-Addes–inspired rumor that some of Reuther's backers from southern and border state locals were members of the Ku Klux Klan, were all too common.

During the voting, tension mounted as the clerk read for four hours through the list of hundreds of locals in the only closely contested presidential election in the UAW's history. Reuther won by a mere 124 votes (each vote represented approximately 100 members) out of a total of 8,764 (4,444 to 4,320). The bulk of Reuther's support came from the General Motors locals. Both contenders had strength in Ford and Chrysler, with Thomas holding the edge. As a result of Richard Frankensteen's support, Thomas received many votes from aircraft locals, although one of the largest, the Willow Run Local 50, went for Reuther. Although most of the members of the aircraft locals had disappeared because of layoffs, they were, oddly, still eligible to vote. These "ghosts" helped Thomas much more than they did Reuther.

In his acceptance speech, Reuther appealed for unity and spoke briefly of his commitment to the principles of social and reform unionism. The offer of unity in fact extended only to George Addes, who was not opposed by the Reuther caucus for reelection as secretary-treasurer. The Reutherites, however, nominated candidates for both vice-presidencies and for all the executive board seats. Here they suffered a sharp setback.

Thomas was elected first vice-president and a Thomas ally, Richard Leonard, was chosen second vice-president. On the board the Thomas-Addes forces gained a two-to-one majority. The opposition, far from routed, had isolated and surrounded Reuther in the presidency.

As soon as one campaign ended, the next began. The division kept the UAW in turmoil until the convention of November 1947. During those twenty months neither side overlooked any step that promised an advantage. Both realized that it was winner take all. As Bill McKie, the Communist activist in Local 600, had predicted earlier: "Sooner or later either the Reuther gang or the Addes side will be in full control of the UAW."

Reuther quickly learned that he did not control the union. The executive board approved policies with which he disagreed, condemned him in resolutions, and even excluded him from some of its meetings. The Thomas-Addes group made effective use of its control of the *United Auto Worker*, the union's paper. Reuther attacked his board opponents as the "mechanical majority"; his friend Eleanor Roosevelt, in her syndicated newspaper column, wrote that the board's public attacks, launched without informing him of the charges, showed "human nature at its worst." Nevertheless, he was able to have his way on some matters. Most important were the appointments of Victor Reuther as head of the Education Department and of Frank Winn as director of publicity. The Education Department became the spearhead of Reuther's offensive. Its summer programs put supporters through a crash course in parliamentary procedure, public speaking, and other useful skills in preparation for the showdown.

Never before or since has the union been caught up in such sustained, intense debate. The leaders of both sides seized every opportunity to speak before important locals. Elections in the locals were closely watched for their bearing on the struggle. When Thomas's home local, the 10,000-member Chrysler Local 7 on Detroit's East Side, chose a slate of officers committed to Reuther with an unusually high turnout of over 70 percent, the tremors were felt throughout the union. Election stunts by both sides enlivened the proceedings. During a vote for officers at Ford Local 600, one right-wing member, dressed in a Soviet uniform with a giant papier-mâché head of Stalin, passed out leaflets urging a vote for the left-wing slate.

In the spring of 1947 the Thomas-Addes faction hatched a plot that they expected to bring victory. They proposed to incorporate the Farm Equipment Workers Union (FE), with which the UAW had long disputed an overlapping jurisdiction among agricultural implement workers, into the UAW. It seemed logical to unite through a merger, with the UAW absorbing the FE membership of about 35,000; but there were two catches. The FE had a left-wing leadership, so the convention votes of the new members would go to the Thomas-Addes faction. More serious, under the terms of the merger, the FE locals would receive 500 convention votes, many more than they were entitled to by their number, and probably enough to put the union under Thomas-Addes control. In short, the FE merger would pack the convention with an anti-Reuther majority.

The proposal was sprung without warning at a board meeting and a resolution approving it passed, but the resolution's backers accepted an amendment calling for a membership referendum. Reuther threw himself into a life-or-death struggle, rushing to locals across the country and debating both Thomas and Addes at noisy, jammed meetings. Far from representing labor unity, he charged, the plan would create a privileged elite. FE would become a semiautonomous union within the UAW; its example would inspire others, such as skilled workers, to claim similar status. Before long the UAW would be irreparably split and destroyed. The proposal lost by a margin of more than two to one. Particularly disturbing to the Thomas-Addes group was its defeat in many locals that had previously been faithful followers.

Desperation drove them to extremes. The board forbade the release of reports by UAW departments without obtaining prior approval, an attempt to gag Reuther's supporters and protect the Thomas-Addes faction from criticism. Reuther became the target of a barrage of false charges that undermined the credibility of those who brought them. One was the publication of a comic book pamphlet entitled *The Bosses' Boy*, produced at union expense by a recently hired publicity man, in which Reuther was portrayed as a company stooge who had consistently betrayed the workers. Another smear was a fabricated letter purportedly written by the Reverend Gerald L. K. Smith, a noisy, anti-Semitic quasi-fascist who praised Reuther for doing an "excellent job" in opposing the union's left wing but cautioned that any public statement of support by Smith would limit Reuther's "sensational usefulness." The most ludicrous smear was a rumor, spread by the columnist Drew Pearson, that Reuther would run for the vice-presidency of the United States on a ticket headed by Senator Robert A. Taft, coauthor of the hated Taft-Hartley Act. Thomas-Addes henchmen supplied UAW local newspapers with an editorial based on the story, and the executive board suggested that the law should be renamed the Taft-Hartley-Reuther Act.

In calmer times a different point of view prevailed. In a 1965 interview after his retirement, R. J. Thomas expressed regret for the unfair attacks and conceded that it "was probably a good thing for the union" that Reuther's reelection had ended destructive factionalism.

Reuther responded to his opponents' campaign with counterstatements, denials, and libel suits. He issued a long statement to the membership presenting an effective combination of positive proposals for improving the union, such as providing verbatim records of board meetings and establishing a board of trustees to ensure fiscal integrity, and attacks on his opponents as the source of disunity and the channel for "outside interference" in union affairs. Using the slogan, "Teamwork in the leadership and solidarity in the ranks," the Reuther forces promised an end to factional battles.

The outcome was decided with the delegate elections. The results showed Reuther a clear winner, the only remaining question being whether any of his opponents would survive. The Reuther caucus, rejecting a request from Murray to make an exception for Addes, decided to run candidates for every office. The opposition was so soundly whipped that it put up no candidate for president. Two token unknowns ran against him, gathering only 339 votes to his 5,593. The real measure of remaining opposition was the 1,219 delegates who abstained and an undetermined portion of the 344 who failed to answer the roll call. The results of the other races were equally decisive. Emil Mazey—a Reuther supporter; former president of Briggs Local 212; and a militant unionist, strike leader, and socialist— bested Addes for secretary-treasurer by nearly a two-to-one margin. Two Reuther backers disposed of Thomas and Leonard for the vice-presidencies, and the Reuther forces won a solid eighteen-to-four control of the board. Mrs. Eleanor Roosevelt greeted the sweep as a heartening development and acclaimed Reuther as a labor leader "who gives us hope for a sane and wise leadership both in labor and in the liberal movement."

The victory of the right-wing caucus had important consequences for the labor movement and liberal politics. The defeat of the Thomas-Addes faction was the key to a series of postwar setbacks for the Communist-cooperating left that soon led to its virtual disappearance from union and public life. The UAW's left-wing element, neither shop floor revolutionaries nor social utopians, was fatally handicapped by the Soviet connection, which had repeatedly put it at odds with the workers' interests and with compelling currents of public opinion and had threatened future costly conflicts. Reuther persuaded the UAW's members that the costs of "outside interference" far exceeded any benefits; in the process, like any practical politician, he had solidified his hold on power and the presidency. His foes' countercharge that Reuther was equally dependent on outside interference—because the ACTU represented the Catholic Church and the Reuther faction was in thrall to the Democratic party—fell flat, since nearly all of the rank and file were Democrats and many were Catholics. The comparison only demonstrated the left's difficulty in perceiving the true character of the ordinary worker's beliefs.

It was fitting that Reuther concluded the convention by introducing his father, "an old soap boxer, an old rabble-rouser . . . an old fighter in the ranks of labor," to the delegates. Val Reuther's brief, stirring address brought them to their feet, and a motion from the floor to make him an honorary UAW member passed by acclamation. No rite could have better confirmed that Walter, a faithful son, had proved worthy of his birthright.

VII

The Democratic Left

WITH HIS DECISIVE VICTORY in the UAW, Reuther became the key figure in constructing an independent, democratic left. It seemed inevitable that the left would be on the defensive in the near future. The pendulum was swinging away from New Deal liberalism and to the extreme right as a result of the domestic pressures generated by the Cold War. The left would have to defend established positions, rather than advance to new ones. The immediate need was to end infighting within the left and the labor movement, uniting on a liberal, noncommunist position that could be held against common enemies.

After the convention Reuther moved quickly to consolidate his position. None of the defeated officers remained active in the union. R. J. Thomas moved to a CIO staff position; Richard Leonard, after a sojourn in a DeSoto factory, followed him into the same haven. George Addes ran a tavern for a time and then became a manufacturer's agent. Richard Frankensteen had left the union earlier to pursue interests in politics and business. Maurice Sugar, the union's counsel for ten years and its highest-paid official, was replaced. Close to the Communists and an aggressive strategist in the factional battle, Sugar had been commonly considered the behind-the-scenes mastermind of the Thomas-Addes faction. Reuther gave no quarter to the opposition leaders, most of whom neither expected nor asked for any, since they knew that in his position they would have acted similarly.

Faithful supporters were rewarded with the jobs of more than a hundred dismissed opposition staff members. Reuther did not remove all who had been against him, however. He recognized the reluctance of nearly all staffers to return to the shop. Since for many of them union jobs had been the only realistic means of upward mobility, a forced return to the factory would sow resentment and the seeds of future opposition. Thus patronage was used to shift as well as to reward loyalty. As one staffer later explained, "We got bought off. . . . What kind of a fool would I be if I didn't accept Walter's offer? At my age and with my broken health, how long would I last if I went back to the Dodge paint shop?"

A damaging though unintended consequence of the Reuther victory was a diminished role for blacks in the UAW's hierarchy. Although Reuther had some black support, most of the activist blacks were associated with the Thomas-Addes group. By the rules of politics, Reuther owed them nothing. Although he later gave staff appointments to some of the better-known blacks once active in the opposition, such as Shelton Tappes of Local 600, the Reuther victory delayed by several years the emergence of a black leadership to correspond with the increasing number of black unionists.

Reuther's reelection as UAW president soon had repercussions throughout the labor movement, bringing on a showdown with the CIO unions that had regularly defended Soviet policies. These were no negligible force, since they represented about 20 percent of the CIO's 6 million members. Only scattered handfuls of the members and a few of those in the leadership were actually Communist party members. In only one of the eleven unions that eventually were expelled from the CIO, the Fur and Leather Workers, were the top leaders avowed Communists. Others may have concealed their membership, or have been former members or fellow travelers who had never joined the party but defended its positions and accepted its direction to some degree. Whatever their status, their organizations had a history of supporting the twists and turns of Communist party positions at least since the Nazi-Soviet pact of 1939.

Foreign policy issues of the Cold War brought a new urgency

to the issue of Communist sympathizers in American labor. To rebuild the economy of war-torn Europe and construct a barrier to the USSR's westward penetration beyond the boundaries of its emerging eastern European satellites, the United States in 1947 proposed the Marshall Plan, consisting of nearly $20 billion in economic aid. The Soviet government reacted with hostility; and American Communists and fellow travelers, including those in CIO unions, dutifully condemned the Marshall Plan as another instance of United States imperialism. To Reuther, whose concern with the fate of labor in western Europe could be traced back to his witness of Hitler's destruction of the German trade unions, these condemnations betrayed the very cause of free unions for which American unionists claimed to stand. He believed the United States had to encourage the development of stable, open economies abroad in which free unions could take root and flourish.

In addition, domestic setbacks and the threat of worse to come made labor unity imperative. In 1947, over President Truman's veto, Congress passed the Taft-Hartley Act, a series of major amendments to the Wagner Act. A complex measure, Taft-Hartley tilted the balance in industrial relations in management's favor, enhanced the states' powers to impede union organizing, and revived the federal government's authority to obtain injunctions to delay strikes in certain circumstances. Furthermore, the law singled out union officers as being of dubious loyalty by requiring them to sign affidavits stating that they were not members of the Communist party. Refusal to sign carried no criminal penalty (although a perjured statement did); but unions whose officers failed to comply would be deprived of certification under the Wagner Act and denied the right to appear before the National Labor Relations Board, which crippled them in dealing with other unions and with management. Their union would become vulnerable to raiding by rivals, and companies could refuse to bargain with them. Branding the law a "slave labor act," organized labor sought its repeal, a goal to which President Truman was also pledged. Even with united labor support, the odds for repeal were unfavorable; without it, they were impossible.

As the election of 1948 approached, the Democratic party seemed about to disintegrate. It had lost control of Congress to the Republicans in the midterm elections of 1946. Southern Democrats were unhappy and restless as their northern colleagues came out in favor of civil rights legislation. A portion of the party's left wing, dissatisfied with Truman's militant Cold War stance and rhetoric, was preparing to break away. The party needed rejuvenation and new leadership in order to defend the gains of the New Deal and go forward from them.

Reuther had moved toward the Democrats for years but still kept his distance. There had always been third-party sentiment within the labor movement, based on the view that both major parties, hopelessly dominated by capitalist interests, failed to represent labor. The surge of labor-based parties in Europe and Canada after the war encouraged the belief that a new American political organization was viable. In late 1945 Victor Reuther claimed that "the time is now ripe for labor to divorce itself from the two old parties and resolve to build the base for an independent, indigenous, new national political party." Walter was less optimistic about a new party's prospects, but he did want to engineer a political realignment that would unite the liberal Democrats and progressive Republicans in one party and the conservatives from both parties in the other. An American national party, he recognized, had to be built on a coalition of class and interest groups. "In Europe," he wrote, "labor parties are a natural political expression because there you have a highly fixed . . . class society. But America is a society in which social groups are in flux, in which you do not have this rigid class structure." Consequently, the labor movement had to seek alliances with small businessmen, farmers, consumers, and minority groups. Although compromises would have to be made, the interests of these groups were sufficiently close that no principle need be sacrificed. Only through added numbers could anything be accomplished.

In January 1947 Reuther and other liberals met in Washington, D.C., at the invitation of Reinhold Neibuhr, the Protestant theologian and liberal activist, to found Americans for Democratic Action (ADA) with the intent of mobilizing the "enormous forces in American life which are both progressive and non-Communist." A particularly disturbing recent event lent urgency to the task. The congressional elections of only two months before had featured red-baiting of liberal candidates, by Richard M. Nixon among others, resulting in defeat for many of them. Unless liberals could persuade the public of their opposition to communism, the future of liberal causes looked bleak. ADA was issue oriented, with the purpose of developing, publicizing, and promoting a liberal position on all public questions. Communism, ADA members believed, was, along with Nazism and fascism, the totalitarian opposite of liberal democracy. Hence ADA excluded Communist party members and fellow travelers from its offices and condemned communism in its charter. In part ADA was founded in response to Progressive Citizens of America—a recently established organization that worked with the Communists and eventually supported Henry Wallace's 1948 campaign for the presidency—to show that the American left was not a Communist captive. With Reuther's backing, the UAW became ADA's financial mainstay, donating $10,000 in the spring of 1948 and making regular contributions thereafter. As a liberal-labor, noncommunist coalition, operating on the left of the Democratic party, ADA was Reuther's most comfortable and enduring political affiliation.

The 1948 election posed an awkward dilemma for Reuther and other ADA liberals. Truman, a man "with his heart in the right place but a man not adequate for the job he inherited," as Reuther had told a reporter, was simply not of presidential stature. His floundering on reconversion, inflation, labor strife, and the removal of price controls confirmed Reuther's judgment; and the president only partly redeemed himself by vetoing the Taft-Hartley Act. He had surrounded himself with cronies and conservative businessmen and had shown neither the liberal vision nor the political skills needed to hold the Democratic party on Roosevelt's course. If Truman ran for reelection, Reuther feared, his loss would drag down the liberal senators and congressmen on whom the UAW and other unions depended. Although dumping an incumbent president defied conventional political wisdom, ADA leaders began to search for an alternative. Reuther preferred Supreme Court Justice William O. Douglas, a New Dealer and a favorite of Roosevelt's, but politically weak. Others in ADA liked General Dwight D. Eisenhower, whose political positions were then unknown but whose popularity was enormous. Expressing what was, perhaps, a wish for a combination of the virtues of each, the ADA board adopted a compromise resolution favoring Eisenhower "and/or" Douglas for the Democratic nomination. When Eisenhower stated he would not accept the nomination if offered, the dump-Truman movement collapsed.

The crisis in politics and in the CIO came to a head when eleven CIO unions, defying the endorsement of Truman by the CIO's Political Action Committee, its political arm, decided to support the candidacy of Henry Wallace, the former vice-president and cabinet member, for the presidency on the new Progressive party ticket. The Wallace movement was backed by American Communists and their sympathizers as well as by some noncommunist liberals. For a serious run at the office, Wallace needed CIO support. Murray and Reuther, however, were suspicious of Wallace and his entourage and realized he had no chance of winning. Worst of all, merely by running Wallace would split the labor-liberal vote, defeating the Democratic candidate and throwing the election to the Republican, Thomas E. Dewey. Thus any success enjoyed by Wallace and other Progressive party candidates would be at the expense of liberal Democrats, and with their defeat would go down any hope of repealing Taft-Hartley and of defending labor against even more restrictive legislation.

Like many labor leaders and professional politicians, Reuther had never trusted Wallace's judgment. Questioned by a reporter about his candidacy, Reuther responded with contempt. "Wallace has become a lost soul. . . . The Communists are doing for him what they do for any other important figure they can bring under their wing." He enumerated their good deeds: "They furnish a complete political valet service; they will write your speeches; they will do your thinking for you; they will arrange and take you to meetings; they will supply the audiences and lead the cheering; and when necessary, to keep you in camp, they will inflate your ego."

Eventually Truman was endorsed by the CIO and the UAW with little enthusiasm and less hope. Since nearly everyone except the candidate expected him to lose, the UAW concentrated its resources on the congressional campaigns. Meanwhile, Reuther and the UAW board, believing the Democratic party was falling apart, proposed a liberal realignment in a new party of workers, farmers, professionals, and small businessmen who wanted a society of economic security and democratic freedoms. The new party would "advocate a program of full production and full employment based on democratic controls in every area of our economic life where the public interest is directly and vitally at stake." Truman's anticipated defeat by Dewey, and a modest showing by Henry Wallace, might lead to a political reshuffle bringing all liberal forces together by 1952.

Truman upset these calculations by winning. Reuther was delighted that so many of the candidates endorsed by the CIO-PAC and ADA for Senate and House seats had been elected, but he said little about the president's victory. With a Democratic president in office and Democratic majorities in both houses of Congress, Reuther's plan for a liberal political realignment was stillborn. The solid failure of Wallace's presidential bid ended the possibility of a split on the left, and the walkout of the Dixiecrats from the Democratic party's convention allowed the Democrats to adopt a civil rights program acceptable to liberals. With the labor movement hopeful for repeal of Taft-Hartley and a resumption of the onward march of the New Deal through new employment security, health insurance, and public housing legislation, Truman's reelection bound labor more firmly than ever to the Democratic party.

At the CIO convention following the election, scores were settled with the dissident unions that had supported Wallace. They were put on trial on charges of disloyalty to the CIO, with expulsion as the penalty for the guilty. The specific tests were support for Communist party positions on a series of political issues ranging from the Nazi-Soviet pact of 1939 to the recent Wallace campaign. The result was the expulsion of eleven unions, including the United Electrical Workers, at the time the third-largest organization in the CIO and Reuther's antagonist in the GM strike.

Most of the expelled unions collapsed within a few years, but the larger and stronger such as UE continued to play an important though diminished role in the labor movement. In several instances the CIO chartered new unions to challenge those that were expelled. Some CIO unions, including the UAW, went after locals within the expelled unions. Some of these locals were dissidents that wanted to escape from their Communist-dominated internationals, but others resisted the UAW's raiding campaign. Since the officers of most of the expelled unions had, for the time being, refused to sign the Taft-Hartley affidavits, they were at a serious disadvantage in retaining their members through NLRB certification elections (their supporters had to vote for "no union" on the NLRB ballot). In this way the UAW picked up most of the members of the expelled Farm Equipment Workers, incorporating their locals into its Agricultural Implements Department. Thus the two unions were brought together on Reuther's terms rather than those previously proposed by the Thomas-Addes faction.

Although he was totally opposed to Communist denials of freedom, Reuther was never drawn to the simplistic and self-defeating position that mere anticommunism, with support for anyone and everyone who proclaimed opposition to the Soviets, was an adequate foreign policy. He frequently criticized both the AFL and the United States government for a blind anticommunism that failed to distinguish between democratic and authoritarian regimes. As he said in a 1948 speech: "the chief weakness of American foreign policy is the predilection of our State Department for dealing with anybody who will promise to hate Communism. It is fatal to resist Communism by courting reaction." Always, he believed, both United States foreign policy and trade union objectives in foreign countries should aim for the positive results that would flow from a free economy and society. The greatest contribution American labor could make to a prosperous and peaceful future was to support the aspirations of workers everywhere to independent, responsible unions of their choice.

The international stance and activities of the labor movement were important aspects of the reconstruction of postwar Europe. As a labor internationalist, Reuther was convinced that workers everywhere must advance together in freedom. To render aid and encourage free trade-union growth, the CIO and labor federations from many countries sent delegations to the founding convention of the World Federation of Trade Unions (WFTU) in 1945. The AFL refused to participate, arguing that the Soviet unions represented in WFTU were instruments of the state rather than free organizations. The CIO, then hopeful of continuing wartime cooperation with the USSR, believed an experiment that included the Soviets in the WFTU was worth trying. From the beginning, however, the organization was troubled by East-West differences. It split when the United States proposed European economic recovery through the Marshall Plan. The USSR condemned the plan and called on Communist-led unions in Italy and France to oppose it. Crippling strikes broke out in those countries; and by the spring of 1949 the CIO had withdrawn from the WFTU, followed by all the major European labor federations except those in France and Italy that were under Communist control.

Later that year a new organization, the International Confederation of Free Trade Unions (ICFTU), was formed with both CIO and AFL participation. Reuther was a CIO delegate to its first convention and served as chairman of a committee that drew up its manifesto on the basic rights to "bread, peace, and freedom." He also participated in the difficult task of drafting a constitution that would give the European trade unions, with their different religious and secular orientations, equal and full rights in the new organization. This required both a skilled negotiator's delicate touch and an unusual sensitivity to national, cultural, and philosophical differences. Reuther had to guard against the attempts of the AFL, which ran an active and relatively well financed operation in Europe, to turn the ICFTU into a rigid anticommunist bloc with little program beyond opposition to the USSR.

Reuther also became active in the International Metal Workers Federation (IMF), an organization supported for years by European metalworkers' unions but with little following in the United States. In 1949 the UAW joined the IMF in order to have "an opportunity to work with representatives of the free labor movement throughout the world in developing a program to protect the working conditions, the wage standards, and general interests of the workers in these basic industries." Reuther agreed to direct a new World Automotive Department within the IMF. Many European trade unionists were skeptical of American leadership, but at an IMF convention in Zurich Reuther won them over with his progressive social and economic ideas. Setting out a broad plan for free trade, recovery assistance, and establishment of international standards in working conditions, he told the delegates, in a characteristic expression of his social democratic philosophy, that "neither Communism nor Wall Street is the solution to our problems."

Although the powers of the World Automotive Department were limited, its establishment was a fortunate development in view of the growth of multinational automotive firms. Reuther's first project was to sponsor a groundbreaking study of automotive contracts around the world in order that unions entering into negotiations might know what their colleagues elsewhere had won. The information was invaluable in formulating demands and conducting negotiations. The department also organized training sessions for union activists and, in general, pursued all means whereby the experiences of workers in one nation could be brought to the aid of others. Eventually, in recognition of the worldwide operations of the giant automotive firms, world councils to facilitate exchanges of information were established within the department for employees of General Motors, Ford, Chrysler, Volkswagen, and other multinational companies. No American union leader of the postwar period was more active than Reuther in promoting international contacts and cooperation among free workers and their organizations.

Reuther's commitment to helping the struggling free unions of Western Europe involved him in an episode in the early 1950s that caused embarrassment when it was revealed in 1967. Victor Reuther was attached to the CIO's international affairs office with responsibility for encouraging the growth of noncommunist trade unions. Since Communist-controlled unions provided strong competition, this was an important and delicate task. The CIA asked the Reuthers, who "reluctantly" agreed, to expend $50,000 of the agency's funds through the CIO for support of anticommunist unions. A CIA agent, who later revealed the Reuthers' involvement, brought the money in small bills to Walter's office for transfer to Victor, who saw to its distribution among democratic trade unions in France and Italy. Apparently the CIA wished to enlist the Reuthers into its apparatus; they refused, however, fearing that their own and their organizations' reputations would be compromised if they became government agents.

In the midst of these activities, Reuther had a close call with death on the night of April 20, 1948, when he barely escaped assassination. He had returned from an evening union meeting and was finishing a late dinner. As he stood in the kitchen, removing a bowl of fruit from the refrigerator, a twelve-gauge shotgun loaded with heavy double-0 buckshot was discharged through a window a few feet away. Only a quick turn at the moment the shot was fired, which allowed his right arm instead of his chest to take the brunt of the blast, saved his life. As it was, his arm was shattered and nearly severed. The arm's nerves were in shreds, and doctors feared that he would never recover its use. Intricate surgery and years of physical rehabilitation eventually led to partial restoration, although his arm never regained full strength.

Thirteen months later Victor Reuther was shot through the living room window of his home in Detroit. The shotgun blast took out his right eye. The two shootings drastically changed the family's lives. Thereafter, Walter was always accompanied by an armed bodyguard. Other members of his family were also protected for a time. Walter sold his home in Detroit and sought more secure surroundings, finally moving to a fenced and guarded, modest but attractive country home thirty-five miles north of Detroit. The UAW bought a bulletproof Packard limousine to replace Reuther's 1940 Chevrolet. Although he was embarrased by riding in a $12,000 automobile, the union insisted that he use it. Reuther's mother, visiting her son in the hospital, gently suggested that he should return to the tool and die trade; but Walter refused. Victor, ravaged even more than Walter by his assault, lived abroad for several years after his recovery, taking a position with the CIO's international affairs division in Paris.

Although the largest rewards in United States history up to that time were offered, mainly by the UAW, neither crime was solved. Investigations were carried on as late as 1968, and the state of Michigan extended the statute of limitations when it appeared that there might be a break in the case. The Detroit police department, no friend of the union, bumbled through a negligent pseudoinvestigation of comic and near criminal proportions. Witnesses and material evidence disappeared from police custody, and investigators hired by the UAW found the police uncooperative. Federal authorities were no more helpful. FBI director J. Edgar Hoover, privately pressed to enter the case, replied that the agency could not become involved "every time a nigger woman gets raped." Among official bodies, only the

Senate's Kefauver committee made anything like a serious attempt to get to the bottom of the crime, but its resources and jurisdiction were limited. The underlying attitude of some of the law enforcement agencies and the newspapers was that the shootings were the work of rival labor gangs trying to bump each other off; the sooner they succeeded, the better.

Many rumors and hypotheses were aired. The favorite with the police was that either the Communists or some other factional rivals within the UAW were responsible. A lack of evidence did not deter them from pushing this theory. The Michigan Communist party, perhaps to deflect police and public attention, contributed $500 to the reward fund. Although many questions remain, the most plausible suspicions center on a gang of East Side Detroit criminals involved in a variety of illegal activities, including union busting. In one of their ploys, they made a lucrative deal for scrap disposal with a factory, which was then subcontracted out to a legitimate disposal firm. For their pay the gang, by using threats, blackjacks, lead pipes, or anything else handy, insured that no union was organized. Around the time of the shootings, the gang tried to move in on workers at the Briggs Manufacturing Company, perhaps at the invitation of some Briggs officials. In any event, a man named Donald Ritchie, after insisting that a portion of the reward money be paid to a girlfriend in Canada, signed a confession stating that he witnessed the shooting by one of the mobsters and was an accomplice himself. Presumably the object was to intimidate the workers by killing Reuther and then open the plants to criminal infiltration. Ritchie escaped from a Detroit hotel where he was being loosely held by Detroit detectives prior to a court appearance. Soon after, he turned up in Canada, repudiated his confession, and went on a spree with the reward money.

Although factional differences did not entirely disappear following Reuther's election in 1947, they ceased to be a preoccupation. Even though pockets of dissent remained, and ambitious men were available to head up a challenge, the general acceptance of the Reuther administration's aims and achievements by the rank and file provided thin soil for the growth of an opposition. Never one to leave matters to chance, Reuther took firm countermeasures where hostility persisted, as at Ford Local 600. There, following an investigation by the House Un-American Activities Committee, he imposed an administratorship for a time that temporarily suspended the local's officers and led to the expulsion of several Communist local functionaries from the union. Although the resultant situation was not entirely to Reuther's liking, he effectively contained a potential challenge to his leadership.

Some of Reuther's critics charged that the decline of factionalism marked the end of democracy in the UAW. The union, they said, ceased to be democratic when it no longer resembled a two-party political system with power passing from one group to the other. The comparison was not persuasive, however, since the structure of power in the union had never been based on two rival parties. A better model was that of competing feudal lords, each with a following and in many cases a program, creating and dissolving combinations as some amalgam of principle and interest dictated.

Furthermore, the two-party test was unrealistic. Only in rare and special circumstances have unions—let alone corporations, schools, universities, armies, or other institutions that normally exist within democratic political systems—made decisions through rival parties. The UAW was almost unique in maintaining a rough balance among several competing groups for as long as it did. The question of democracy in trade unions, as in these other institutions, turns on the responsiveness of the leadership to the aspirations and needs of those it serves. Lines of communication must be open, with decisions based on discussion and consensus. Most important, the leadership cannot maintain itself in power by unscrupulous or strong-arm methods that render it immune to critics or opposition. The Reuther administration of the UAW met these tests. Two years after Reuther's election, the columnist Murray Kempton wrote in *The New York Post* that Reuther had "very carefully and conspicuously not done what so many of us thought he would do—turn the UAW into an iron personal machine." The UAW under Reuther had fewer dramatic confrontations and operated in a much smoother, more bureaucratic style; but it was democratic.

With the deaths of CIO president Philip Murray and William Green, president of the AFL, in late 1952, Reuther became the most influential labor figure in the country. The two candidates for the CIO presidency were Reuther and Allan Haywood, its executive vice-president and a close associate of Murray's in the steelworkers' union. Haywood, however, was sixty-four years of age; many, including Reuther, believed that David MacDonald, Murray's successor as president of the steelworkers, was promoting Haywood's candidacy merely to block Reuther's election in order that MacDonald himself could gain the office at the next convention. The bitter campaign left a lasting rift between the CIO's two largest unions and their leaders. In the absence of more substantive issues, Reuther himself became one. Several of the heads of other CIO unions were put off by his ambition and his austere personal habits. Labor leaders, they thought, should wait patiently to mount the ladder to higher office; meanwhile, they should join heartily in the customary rounds of good fellowship, card games, and drinking at labor's gatherings. One union president said that he would support Reuther if the auto workers' president would join him for a drink. Reuther obliged, but he did not give a very convincing performance. Haywood, on the other hand, was beloved and respected, a former Yorkshire coal miner whose life had been devoted to labor. His appeal, however, was somewhat offset by MacDonald, a vain man whose manner said that the labor movement was fortunate to have his services. Just before the vote, when a Reuther victory seemed certain, MacDonald, trying to paper over the differences, told Reuther that the contest had a positive result since "at least we have come to like each other better." Reuther's brutal, honest reply, "I would say that we have come to *know* each other better, Dave," cost him the traditional unanimous vote for the winner. Supported by the larger CIO unions, except the steelworkers, Reuther won with 3,078,181 votes to Haywood's 2,613,103. Following the example of Lewis and Murray, his predecessors as CIO presidents, Reuther retained the presidency of his own union, treating the CIO position as part-time and unpaid.

In the long and complicated fight to break the connection between the American left and the USSR, Reuther relied on democratic means of discussion, debate, and freedom of decision. He initially opposed signing the Taft-Hartley affidavits when the question came before the UAW's board. As it became clear, however, that noncompliance would put the union at a serious disadvantage in countering hostile employers and rival unions, particularly the AFL's International Association of Machinists (IAM), and in carrying out organizing campaigns, he took the position that officers should sign under protest. The 1947 convention adopted a Reuther-backed resolution ordering them to do so.

Reuther opposed the use of government power against his opponents or deprivations of their civil liberties. Every member of the union, he wrote, has the "right to believe in his personal political philosophy," but not to impose it on others. Avowed Communists, who were subject to party discipline, should be excluded from union offices; otherwise, he opposed political tests for membership. When Michigan's governor in 1947, at the height of Reuther's reelection campaign, charged before the House Un-American Activities Committee that several UAW officers, excluding Reuther, were captives of communist ideology, Reuther, to the governor's angry surprise, denounced him for unwarranted interference in the union's affairs and "sweeping charges" that smeared innocent people and organizations.

Of greatest importance in that fight was his insistence on the constructive alternative. He stoutly denied that the choices were limited to communism and anticommunism. A third way—a collective welfare state pursued and created through democratic political means and the methods of free unions—was superior to either. The unions and liberal organizations like ADA had to adopt and implement a "basic philosophy . . . to make economic democracy work," consisting of good wages, economic security, adequate housing, and fair employment. Reuther constantly criticized the dangerous tendency of anticommunism to cast aside all restraint and sink into a destructive monomania. "I've been preaching for years," he told a reporter, "that you can't lick the Communists with hysteria. You've got to have a positive program to do the job." In the Cold War decade Reuther sought the path for an independent, democratic left to follow.

VIII

Bargaining Landmarks

THE END OF FACTIONAL STRIFE in the UAW coincided with the dawning of a golden age for the auto industry. Demand for cars seemed insatiable. In 1948 only half of American households owned automobiles; twenty years later the figure had increased to over 80 percent. From 1946 through 1972 American manufacturers built 170 million passenger cars and 35 million trucks and buses. Despite occasional bursts of inflation and decline into recession, the economy produced an unprecedented rise in real incomes. Most Americans chose to spend a substantial portion of their new riches on cars.

Auto manufacturing was the most prosperous of major industries. For nearly every year from 1947 to 1967, the annual rates of return (net profits after taxes divided by net worth) were at least twice as great in the auto industry as in all manufacturing corporations. For those twenty-one years the industry's average annual return was 17 percent, including the losses of firms that failed such as Kaiser-Frazer and Studebaker-Packard, as well as the profits of those that succeeded. The UAW calculated that the profits of the Big Three from 1947 to 1969 were $35 billion— fourteen times their invested capital. No other business matched that record. Since the companies constituted an oligopoly, with no price competition among themselves and little sustained foreign competition in major segments of the market, they simply passed rising labor and other costs through to consumers. The industry was a bonanza for owners, executives, and employees.

To be sure, in time some shadows would be thrown across this sunny landscape. The mass market, dominated by domestic manufacturers since its inception, began to be shared with foreign firms. Volkswagen successfully invaded the United States market in the late 1950s, and Japanese manufacturers followed suit a few years later. Such interest as American companies showed in the small, economical cars the foreign makers produced was confined to marginal firms such as Nash, Kaiser-Frazer, and Crosley. In 1948 Ford and Chevrolet contemplated production of small cars for the American market, but they built and sold them instead in Europe and Australia. As long as they could sell big cars, with their higher profit margins, the companies had little incentive to build small ones. The UAW, whose previous management policy proposals had not been welcomed, urged the manufacturers in 1949 to produce small cars affordable by ordinary workers, pointing out that "a light car can be made cheaply" and would "cost less and conserve national resources." Again, during negotiations in 1958, Reuther raised the question of the suitability of the companies' cars for the market, noting Volkswagen's rising sales, while American cars "every year get longer, the fins get higher, and they put enough horsepower under the hoods to fly them." Not until 1959, when they faced a mounting tide of imports, did the major American manufacturers enter the small car field; even then, their commitment was temporary and halfhearted.

With good times, the public verbal assaults that had marked earlier rounds of bargaining disappeared. All the companies, though still dedicated to tough negotiating and prepared to withstand an occasional strike, accepted the UAW with more grace. They had learned once and for all that workers would stand by the union in a struggle.

New management had a major effect. Most of the executives of the hard-nosed, depression-era generation had passed from the scene. At General Motors Charles E. Wilson replaced Alfred P. Sloan as chairman of the board, and others in the central and plant administration had retired. The role in GM of the

DuPonts, whose holdings came under attack in a tangled and finally successful antitrust suit, was diminished. Although Wilson is best remembered for stating, during Senate hearings on his nomination as secretary of defense in the Eisenhower cabinet, that what's good for General Motors is good for the country, he was imaginative, open-minded, and audacious in labor relations. Some of the workers' contract gains owed more to him than to the union, and a genuine mutual respect developed between the GM chairman and Reuther.

At Ford, too, new personnel improved the atmosphere. The elder Henry Ford and Harry Bennett departed before the war ended, and Henry Ford II brought in a talented management team to lift the ailing company out of the doldrums. The newcomers were prepared to accept and work with the UAW and, in several respects, responded more readily and favorably to the union's demands than did their competitors.

For two decades after 1947 the union charted a pioneer's course in collective bargaining, emerging with pay and other benefit provisions that set a standard for workers everywhere. The objectives were traditional, but many of the means were novel. Workers demanded benefits from advances in productivity brought about through more efficient organization and further automation of production. Automatic cost-of-living increases provided protection against inflation. Retirement income security was guaranteed by pensions that supplemented Social Security. Finally—an objective that was especially important in the seasonal and cyclical auto industry—an income for workers approximating their normal wage was guaranteed throughout the year. Other fringe benefits, especially provision of medical and dental care, were also part of the UAW's program; but the union was not so much the pathbreaker in those kinds of compensation as it was in wage security and retirement income.

Reuther, recuperating from his gunshot wound, played no direct part in the 1948 negotiations with GM, but was kept informed and participated in important decisions. The company took the initiative. Conceding that workers deserved a steadily rising standard of living as the corporation became more efficient and prospered, GM proposed that an annual improvement factor be built into the wage structure. The factor represented each worker's share of rising output per man-hour, based on general expectations of productivity improvements rather than on GM's own performance. For 1948 the proposal called for a 2 percent wage increase, or about 3 cents an hour, in each of the two years of the agreement.

Another major change proposed by the company was a cost-of-living allowance (COLA) that would raise or lower a worker's wage in accordance with price changes as measured by the cost of living index—the first such plan implemented in a mass-production industry. The formula provided that an increase of 1.14 points in the index during a quarter would trigger a pay raise of 1 cent an hour. A decline of the same amount would correspondingly lower wages, although the company agreed to a maximum reduction of 5 cents an hour regardless of how low the index went. With some merit Reuther later claimed that the escalator was a modification of his 1945 proposal to link wages to prices. The improvement factor and COLA increases immediately added 11 cents per hour to the workers' pay.

Labor leaders had long been suspicious of cost-of-living escalators, fearing that they would impose a ceiling above but no floor below wage rates. In view of wage reductions in the depression, the fear was well founded in experience, and at first the GM proposal drew much criticism from the ranks. However, the GM plan met most of the objections, and in any case the future brought inflation, rather than deflation, alternating with periods of price stability. In the first year the COLA raises jumped ahead by 3 cents an hour, then fell back to the original level. Over the years COLA and the annual improvement factor proved their value. In 1948 the straight-time wage, without fringes, averaged $1.50 an hour. By 1980 it was $10.77. Of the increase of $9.27, $5.44 came from COLA and $2.71 from the annual improvement factor, or 75 percent of the total wage. The remainder of the increase, only $1.12 an hour, was attributable to general raises, the correction of inequities, and additions of higher-paid jobs to the work force.

Wilson remained the leading champion of COLA on the industry's side. In 1952 he defended the cost-of-living escalator in terms that Reuther could not have improved on. "The working people," he wrote in a *Reader's Digest* article, "did not make . . . inflation. They only want to catch up with it in order to be able to pay their grocery bills. I contend that present high wages are more the result of fundamental inflationary money pressures than of unreasonable wage pressures by the union." Instead of the "wage-price spiral," he continued, "we should say the 'price-wage spiral.' For it is not primarily wages that push up prices, it is primarily prices that pull up wages." Whatever the facts of the case, it was at least novel for a leading auto executive to exonerate union workers of blame for inflation.

In return for the annual improvement factor and COLA, Wilson wanted a longer-term contract. In fact, both company and union officials realized that annual negotiations were costly. No sooner was a settlement reached than tension over the next year's bargaining began to build. Most serious from the corporation's point of view was the difficulty of long-range planning. Without knowing labor costs in advance, the company had to be cautious and tentative in investing in plants, machinery, and product development. Correctly anticipating strong future demand, Wilson was eager to secure an agreement of at least two years' duration, and he was willing to pay to get it. His position did not endear him to many businessmen (competitors called GM "Generous Motors"), but Wilson went his way and the others had to follow.

A question as pressing as wages was workers' pensions. Security in old age had once been the individual's responsibility. If he failed to save, family or charity were his only recourses. The Social Security pensions originally provided a benefit of $32 a month, too little in the inflationary postwar economy. Most companies took the position that they were not required to

bargain on pensions since the beneficiaries were neither employees nor eligible for full membership in the union. Granting
a pension, they said, was a management prerogative in which the
union had no voice. In 1947 the Ford Motor Company offered
its workers a choice between a contributory pension plan, with
no union participation in its administration, and a wage increase. Although the Ford workers chose wages, the offer
convinced Reuther that, when the time came for the union to
move on pensions, Ford should be the target.

Reuther believed that pensions were a legitimate subject for
bargaining, and he contributed more than anyone else to
gaining acceptance of this view. It was essential, he thought, for
the union to share in the administration and operation of
pension funds. The amounts accumulated by the manufacturers
would be huge and therefore tempting. Employees had to be
protected against a company scheme to raise capital disguised as
a pension plan. Workers who believed their retirement income
was secure had been victimized in the past when there were no
funds to pay their pensions.

Reuther launched a strong campaign to build support in the
union, contrasting the pensions provided to company officials
with the workers' prospects. Pointing out that Chairman Charles
E. Wilson would have a pension of $25,000 a year, although his
annual salary and bonus payments came to $516,000, Reuther
said: "If you make $258 an hour, they give it to you. If you make
$1.65 an hour, they say: 'You don't need it, you're not entitled to
it, and we are not going to give it to you.' " Reuther may have
invented, and certainly popularized, the telling phrase, "too old
to work and too young to die," to dramatize the plight of many
retired workers. As he recalled, he first used it in 1949 at a mass
meeting of 7,000 older Ford employees, where he pledged there
would be no Ford contract without a pension plan. Threatened
with a strike, Ford agreed to pay the entire cost of pensions of
$20 million a year. Ford workers with thirty years' service were
eligible for a pension of $100 a month, three times the amount
then available from Social Security alone. Reuther insisted that

the company actually reserve the funds from which the pensions would be paid; that is, pensions must be fully funded. Furthermore, the plan must be actuarially sound: the amount set aside had to be keyed to the life expectancies of the retirees. Well aware of the uncertainties of the car business, he was on guard against a company that made promises but might not be around to keep them.

The UAW moved on to Chrysler with the pension demand. Chrysler agreed to match the $100-a-month figure but refused to fund the pensions. Reuther insisted on a strike despite evidence that many workers did not understand the issue or appreciate its importance. The strike lasted 104 days, the longest in Chrysler's history. After nearly three months, the company offered to deposit $30 million in the bank as a sign of good faith. Reuther pointed out to a meeting of auto workers that, although this did not amount to funding, it was a step in that direction. "Yeah, Walter," a voice called out from the rear, "but is it actuarially sound?" The financial pitfalls of pensions were sinking in. With both sides making concessions to end the strike, Chrysler agreed to full funding, and GM came through a few weeks later with a pension of $125 a month, including Social Security. The pension reform act of 1974 made funding a requirement for all plans.

The pension plans had an immediate impact. By the end of 1952 nearly 30,000 auto workers had retired with pensions, and the number mounted rapidly. The Gulf Coast of Florida would never be the same. In 1949 the typical monthly retirement income for an auto worker and his wife under Social Security was a mere $54. By the end of the following decade the sum available from Social Security had doubled to $108, but the addition of the negotiated pension brought the total to $245 a month. The UAW's retirement achievement was rounded out in 1964 when Chrysler, followed by GM and Ford, agreed to a $100-a-month early retirement plan without a strike.

In Reuther's view, retirement did not end the members' relationship with the union. Reared in the belief that a worker's class identity lasted a lifetime, he thought that association with the union should also continue. In the 1950s the UAW developed a comprehensive program of social, recreational, political, and community activities that could both replace the role of work for retirees and enable them to contribute to winning the union's public policy objectives.

The success of the UAW and other unions in securing pensions led to increases in Social Security payments that benefited even unorganized workers. Social Security was funded by a payroll tax levied equally on employer and employee; negotiated pensions, however, as in the auto industry, were usually funded solely by the employer. Thus the greater the share of pension costs the employer could shift to Social Security, the less his burden. Employers had successfully opposed any general increase in the Social Security tax since its enactment in 1935, but now their opposition began to fade. With reduced employer opposition, Congress raised payroll taxes, making possible greater benefits for all covered workers.

In 1950 another landmark collective bargaining agreement with General Motors was reached without a strike. The corporation liked the results of the 1948 agreement. Since postwar inflation had leveled off between 1948 and the beginning of the Korean War in June 1950, the costs of the annual improvement factor and COLA were not excessive. Company planning had proceeded smoothly. Now the UAW asked for pensions of $125 a month and other wage improvements. On May 23, 1950, agreement was reached. Workers became eligible for pensions after twenty-five years of employment. The contract raised the annual improvement factor to 4 cents an hour, continued COLA, and included hospitalization and medical care with the company paying half the cost for a worker and his family. The UAW estimated that the settlement was worth 19 cents an hour immediately and would ultimately reach at least 35 cents an hour. A *Detroit News* banner headline read, "Billion Won in GM Pact"—the largest sum in a settlement to that time. The contract also granted a modified union shop, which required new

Production at GM and Ford nearly came to a standstill. Finally, in May 1953, the union prevailed. GM gave production workers a 10 cent raise with an additional 10 cents for skilled workers, revised the cost-of-living formula upward and increased the base rate, raised the annual improvement factor to 5 cents an hour, improved pensions to $137.50 a month, and arranged group health coverage for retirees.

The reopening of the contracts, which the companies resented and made an occasion for considerable moralizing about the sanctity of obligations, would later prove a useful precedent for the auto manufacturers. In 1979, Chrysler, compelled by the federal government as the condition of its loan guarantees, successfully reopened its contract with the UAW in order to erase promised wage increases. GM and Ford later demanded and obtained similar relief through negotiations.

The most daring innovation in compensation was the guaranteed annual wage. The idea was not entirely new, but few experiments had been tried. Auto manufacturing was a challenging place to make a start since it was both a seasonal and a cyclical business, subject to sudden and drastic changes in the level of demand. By the same token, auto workers were most in need of the protection a guaranteed wage could provide. As long ago as 1936, President Roosevelt, campaigning in Detroit, had noted the problem of seasonal and cyclical layoffs in the industry and stated his "belief that the manufacturers of automobiles . . . must, by planning, do far more than they have done to date to increase the yearly earnings of those who work for them."

Reuther began to discuss an annual wage in 1945, warning businessmen that "if private enterprise wants to stay private, it has to stay enterprising. If you won't accept a continuing commitment to employ, the government will have to move in." By 1950 he was ready to make the annual wage a major objective. "It is more than a matter of economic justice to the wage earner," he wrote, "it is a matter of economic necessity to our nation, for freedom and unemployment cannot live together in democracy's house." Posing the question on a personal level, he asked, "Corporation executives get paid by the year—why not a worker?"

Many problems stood in the way of a feasible plan. A major question was whether payments made to temporarily laid-off workers could be combined with unemployment compensation benefits. If a state could reduce unemployment compensation in proportion to privately paid benefits, then a company-funded plan would have no effect on income. In 1951, when Reuther was convinced the idea would work, the union's convention discussed the principles involved and, without a dissenting vote, mandated that it be the next major bargaining goal. Three years later a detailed plan was approved. No major demand advanced by the UAW, or perhaps by any union, was given a more thorough scrutiny.

At the conclusion of the process in 1955, Reuther announced that, although "we are not irrevocably committed to our specific proposal, we are irrevocably committed to the principle that the workers in our industries are morally and economically entitled to a year-round wage." The union's objectives were to give employers an incentive to plan year-round employment, provide income sufficient to maintain living standards for laid-off workers, protect against short work weeks, integrate the annual wage with unemployment compensation, and establish a joint administration of the fund. The convention affirmed the plan and authorized assessments to build a war chest of $25 million, the first large strike fund in the union's history. With the industry headed toward a record production that year of nearly 8 million cars, the companies desperately wished to avoid a strike.

General Motors, as was often the case after Wilson's departure, adopted a rigid position, viewing the annual wage as a challenge to management's control of policies. In a long reply to the union's demand, GM said it was being asked to pay wages for work that was not performed and gloomily predicted the corporation's doom. It countered with a generous financial offer, extending to factory hands a voluntary, subsidized stock purchase plan already available to white-collar workers. As wage protection, GM offered to make interest-free loans on the security of laid-off employees' stock. Reuther reacted strongly. "Hell," he said, "that's for the provident. I'm interested in the folks who can't take care of themselves." GM's unbending response led to a rule of thumb accepted for the remainder of Reuther's presidency: if the UAW wanted money, it went first to GM; but if it had a new idea, it went to Ford.

The negotiations with Ford followed a classic Reuther style, with careful preparation, precise planning, sweet reason, and occasional explosions as circumstances dictated. Believing that Ford would respond with its own counterproposal, Reuther was shocked when the Ford negotiator, John Bugas, began to read the GM stock ownership plan. As Reuther later recalled:

> I said, "John, please don't insult our integrity and your integrity . . . when you know and I know that this is the General Motors Corporation proposal, which we rejected two weeks ago—and you haven't changed a word of it. . . .We do not question your right to stooge for the General Motors company. But I'd like to suggest that it's very bad policy and it will get you nowhere. You guys have got rocks in your head."

Reuther continued, "You have just bought yourself a strike." He went on to recite how a long strike against Willys-Overland had started that company's decline and pointed out that the 1950 strike against Chrysler had prevented it from overtaking Ford in sales. Reminding Bugas that the union had extended its contract with General Motors for the time being, he gibed, "How will you produce Fords on the Chevrolet assembly line?"

Bugas countered by claiming that the workers favored Ford's offer over the union's guaranteed annual wage plan by a margin of nine to one. He insisted that the company had a survey to sustain this point. Reuther, confident of rank-and-file backing, quickly put the claim to the test. "Will you agree to have a referendum vote of Ford workers . . . on our proposal?" he asked. "If they vote for yours, we'll sign a contract containing your proposal. If they vote for ours, we'll sign a contract with that. Since you say they want yours by nine to one, you're not taking any chances." Later, Reuther recalled, "Poor John! I thought he'd die."

Ford did not take up the challenge. It withdrew its offer and proposed a "supplemental unemployment benefits" (SUB) plan, which accepted the union's position as the basis for settlement. Much hard bargaining lay ahead, however, since Ford's original proposal was a far cry from the union's idea of wage security. Even with further threats of a strike, Ford would yield only so much. Eventually, the company agreed to put 5 cents an hour for each worker into a SUB trust fund totaling $5.5 million that would be drawn on to provide payments of $25 a week for up to twenty-six weeks for laid-off workers. When unemployment compensation was added, a worker would receive 65 percent of take-home pay for the first four weeks of layoff and 60 percent for the next twenty-two weeks. With only twenty-six weeks covered, the original SUB plan was a semiannual rather than an annual guaranteed wage. Reuther, however, regarded it as merely the first step.

GM executives remained opposed to the SUB plan, but they wanted no part of a strike when sales were booming. After a week of hard bargaining, GM accepted the Ford contract. The company did not approve but felt it had to accept.

The SUB plan soon proved its value. During the first three years, from 1956 to 1959, more than $105 million was paid out, mostly during the recession of 1958 when car sales dried up, the national unemployment rate rose to more than 7 percent, and hundreds of thousands of auto workers were laid off. Reuther made increased SUB funding and extensions of benefits priority bargaining items. In 1967, following a two-month strike at Ford, when a laid-off worker received 95 percent of take home pay for up to fifty-two weeks, less a $7.50 weekly deduction for savings in commuting and lunch costs, SUB became a genuine annual wage guarantee. Benefits at that level could create an incentive for layoff, although that was not so often the case as employment in the 1970s became less secure. The prolonged layoffs that followed the OPEC embargo on oil shipments in 1973–1974 and subsequent oil price increases showed that the SUB well could run dry. Neither Ford nor Chrysler replenished the fund sufficiently to maintain the contracted level of benefits, although both funds recovered when full production resumed. SUB provided a new degree of income security in an industry notorious for irregular earnings.

In 1961 a profit-sharing plan was instituted at American Motors (AMC). Because of its financial weakness, the UAW did not hold AMC to the contract terms negotiated with the Big Three. Profit sharing would reward workers if the company prospered but would not saddle AMC with high costs if profits failed to materialize. A sum equal to 15 percent of the profits was used to set up a workers' fund. One-third of that bought AMC stock for employees; the rest financed pensions, insurance, and supplemental unemployment payments.

Less attention was given to working conditions than to wages and pensions, but they were not ignored. Although Reuther concentrated on money issues in national talks, supplementary agreements on conditions were hammered out at each plant. In the 1960s working conditions became a more significant national issue. Particularly troublesome at GM in 1961 was the inadequate relief time given to line workers to go to rest rooms, which led to the brief "toilet strike."

The auto talks were the major leagues of bargaining. The periodic encounters between Reuther and the car companies captured public attention in the postwar decades. Except for the strike of 1945–1946, Reuther's conduct of negotiations was rarely criticized. Employing all the arts and ploys of the negotiator, from the humdrum to the dramatic, and even inventing some new ones, Reuther masterfully played the bargaining game.

Both skilled in publicity and mindful of the need for public and union support, Reuther began negotiations with a presentation designed to rally the troops, win public approval, and put the companies on the defensive. Weeks before the contracts expired, trailed by a small army of aides, he went from company to company for an opening session, dominating the meetings with a long and emotional exposition of the union's demands, bristling with assertions of the workers' militancy. The companies had to be convinced that the union would strike, but kept in the dark as to the exact concessions that would prevent one. At these affairs company representatives made little attempt to upstage Reuther. They sat back to watch the show, content to make restrained and often condescending responses.

Once the talks began, Reuther took little direct part until the deadline approached and a strike loomed. In the meantime, with issues assigned to joint committees, subordinates on both sides moved along with lesser matters, leaving the money settlement and major innovations, if any, for the principals.

In the small group that came together as negotiations moved toward a conclusion, Reuther made no speeches, becoming strictly a tough and resourceful bargainer. As one GM official said, "There are two kinds of Walter Reuthers, the Reuther we deal with, and a second Reuther who's out throwing punches before the public." He was quick to discern chinks in the enemy's armor and to turn any unexpected development to account. In September 1955 difficult negotiations with GM coincided with Reuther's birthday. Louis Seaton, GM vice-president and chief negotiator, presented him with a cake; but the reporters covering the talks provided another, larger one. "Like the GM offer," Reuther told them, "Mr. Seaton's cake was inadequate." The traditional way to conclude talks was in a marathon session carried down to the deadline. Reuther, who rejuvenated himself with periodic tooth scrubbings during long sessions, tipped off reporters that he expected a marathon and a settlement by bringing his toothbrush to the bargaining table.

Reuther's mental and physical energy and his stamina—the result of a lifetime of exercise, regular habits, abstinence from alcohol and tobacco, and a fine physical and mental constitution—paid off at the bargaining table. His skill at tense, high-stakes bargaining was fully appreciated in the UAW. Coming out of a session a few hours before a strike deadline, he discovered some UAW colleagues happily playing cards. "How can you characters sit there and play poker and have a damned good time," he asked, "and we're six hours away from a possible strike?" One replied, "We just know you'll figure out the answer," and he did.

Reuther had never believed that collective bargaining alone could deal with all the problems of the workers or the nation. Many of the conditions that needed correction in order to establish adequate standards of living could be dealt with comprehensively only through political and government action. During the Eisenhower administration, Reuther was in opposition. He had little respect for Eisenhower and his fellow Republicans, whom he considered indifferent to the needs of ordinary Americans. In 1956, when a short but sharp recession pushed unemployment in the auto industry to 200,000, an Eisenhower aide remarked that "the right to suffer is one of the joys of a free economy." Reuther protested angrily and elicited an apology. The emergence of talented, liberal, Democratic leaders such as Adlai E. Stevenson and John F. Kennedy encouraged Reuther. He strongly supported Stevenson for the Democratic presidential nomination in 1952 and 1956; regretted the unfortunate timing that matched Stevenson against Eisenhower, the unbeatable national hero; and looked forward to renewed progress in economic and social programs under a future Democratic administration.

Reuther was interested in a broad range of projects, and his mind was a fertile source of ideas. A friend once joked that the first copy of his pamphlet on aircraft production came from the press mistitled "500 Plans a Day." Although his reform energies might seem scattered, in fact they were concentrated on housing and health—next to employment and income security the two most important needs of a good society, in Reuther's opinion.

A devoted family man himself, Reuther believed that every worker and his family deserved a comfortable, secure, attractive, and sufficiently spacious home. After World War II he proposed to utilize vacant war plants to mass-produce prefabricated houses. A government corporation similar to the Tennessee Valley Authority should be established to determine which factories could be adapted for the purpose. The facilities could then be operated by that corporation or leased to private manufacturers or workers' cooperatives. In 1945 he wrote that "the same mass production miracles which have made us a nation on wheels can place a modern, durable, healthy home within the economic reach of the common man. . . . The entire vicious circle of primitive methods and restrictive practices in the building industry can be broken." Such words did not endear Reuther to building tradesmen and contractors, but he never conceded that anything less than mass production would solve the problem of outworn, inadequate housing. In 1949, testifying before the Senate as chairman of the CIO National Housing Committee, he stated that two-bedroom houses could be mass-produced for as little as $6,000. In ten years, he predicted, 20 million prefabricated homes could be erected, using a self-replenishing revolving fund that would initially require a government investment of $500 million. Reuther was an advocate of urban renewal—not the kind that replaced tenements with high-speed freeways and luxury apartments, but a renewal that provided ordinary people with decent, affordable housing.

Adequate medical care was as important to Reuther as housing. Since the adoption of Social Security in 1935, many of its advocates had considered a similar national health insurance plan as its logical, necessary extension. In the postwar period the UAW was the country's foremost labor champion of national medical insurance, but the stalemate of political forces prevented public action. Though never conceding that anything less than a national plan would suffice, Reuther and the UAW pursued medical care for auto workers through bargaining. Reuther dramatized the failure of health care with an anecdote about Charles E. Wilson of General Motors. Speaking to a UAW conference on health care in 1949, he told of a young man he met in the hospital while undergoing treatment for his gunshot wound. The man had been paralyzed for nine years but had run out of money just as the treatments were taking effect and had to leave the hospital. Reuther then related the story of Charles E. Wilson's bull, one he often used:

C. E. Wilson had a bull and the bull had a bad back. We are sorry about that. But what happened to C. E. Wilson's bull compared to this boy who was paralyzed for nine years? In the case of C. E. Wilson's bull, the General Electric Company sent a special 140,000-volt X-ray machine into Detroit on a special chartered airplane. It was picked up by a General Motors truck and taken out to C. E. Wilson's farm. The bull didn't even have to leave home to get medical care. Then when they got the 140,000-volt machine there they couldn't operate it because they didn't have enough power, so the Detroit Edison Company ran a special power line out to C. E. Wilson's farm.

Then medical specialists flew in from all over the country and they gave this bull the best medical care that modern medicine and science knows how to deliver. Now why? Why? I ask that simple, honest question. Why did C. E. Wilson's bull get the best of medical care while millions of these kids all over America are not getting that kind of care? It is because C. E. Wilson's bull cost $16,000, and you get boys and workers for free. . . .

With no breakthrough on a public health insurance plan imminent, the UAW tried to persuade management to bargain on company-financed medical benefits. Although Kaiser-Frazer, destined for only a brief life as an auto manufacturer, agreed to a hospitalization and medical program in 1948, not until the NLRB upheld an unfair labor practice charge against General Motors for refusal to bargain did the major manufacturers agree to discuss medical benefits. A major concession came in 1950, when GM agreed to pay half the cost of hospital and surgical coverage for the worker and his family. After Ford and Chrysler followed suit, more than one million UAW members plus their families were covered by plans for which employers paid at least half the cost.

Reuther was never satisfied with the hospitalization and surgical coverage provided by Blue Cross/Blue Shield. It was too limited and made little provision for preventive care or early diagnosis. Blue Cross/Blue Shield, he concluded, because of rising costs, overemphasis on hospitalization and surgery, and indifference to preventive care and outpatient treatment, could meet only about half of the average family's medical bill.

Comprehensive programs, such as the Health Insurance Plan and the Kaiser Health Foundation were available in New York and California, respectively. UAW members in those states could join them. In 1957, at the UAW's prompting, the Community Health Association (CHA) was established to provide prepaid health services in the Detroit area. Reuther, who had once favored a UAW-owned and -operated health service and hospital for its members, came to believe that a community organization, open to any group, was a sounder approach. CHA, which began operations in 1960 with Reuther as president, provided about 35 to 40 percent more in services than Blue Cross/Blue Shield, at about the same cost. Immediate savings were realized through group practice with physicians on salary, and long-run costs were reduced through preventive and outpatient care. Negotiations in 1961 won for most UAW members in the Detroit area the right to choose which plan they preferred; within two years 30,000 had selected CHA.

Among other national questions that affected many citizens as well as auto workers, automation became a serious issue in the 1950s. Some of the new machines could handle routine jobs previously performed by unskilled and semiskilled labor. Others, however, such as automated metal-forming and shaping machines, displaced some of the most skilled workers in the industry. For finishing cylinder heads at one factory in 1949, six machines, representing an investment of $240,000, were required to produce 108 cylinder heads an hour at a labor cost of 20 cents per piece. Five years later a single automatic machine, costing $230,000, reduced the labor cost to 4 cents a piece with the same production.

Reuther never opposed new technology. When asked if he favored a ban on the introduction of new machines, he replied, "Nothing could be more wicked or foolish. You can't stop technological progress and it would be silly to try it if you could." Technology would bring numerous benefits, freeing workers "from the monotonous drudgery of many jobs in which the worker today is no more than a servant of the machine." If handled correctly, new technology would raise the standard of living for all.

The displacement of workers was a problem, however, and its effects could ultimately harm the industry. When Reuther toured a new, highly automated Ford engine plant in Cleveland, a company engineer taunted him with the remark, "You know, not one of those machines pays dues to the United Automobile Workers." Reuther shot back: "And not one of them buys new Ford cars, either." Automation tended to replace routine, low-paying jobs with skilled, well-paying jobs; but, Reuther asked, "*How* does the hand trucker become an electronics engineer—or a skilled technician?" Only a nationally planned and funded program of retraining would be effective. Since all shared the benefits of automation, it was only fair that all share the burden through taxation. Workers deserved to have lost wages replaced during retraining, and those too old to learn a new skill should be offered early retirement. The Eisenhower administration, "looking through a rear-view mirror," as Reuther put it, neglected the need. Under Kennedy and Johnson, however, significant national retraining programs were launched.

In the postwar period the auto workers moved squarely into the middle class as measured by earnings, security of employment and income, medical care, and retirement pensions. In 1947 the annual wage in the auto industry averaged $2,998; by 1958 it had increased to $5,409. Home ownership became more common. Detroit and Flint, the two major centers of manufacturing and assembly, had the highest proportion of owner-occupied homes of any American cities of their size. A fitting symbol of prosperity was the auto worker's own car. Once streetcars and buses had carried most workers to the factory, but now most drove their own cars or light trucks. One reason the car manufacturers began to build new plants on the outskirts of industrial cities was that cheap land was available for parking lots to hold the employees' cars.

Under Reuther's direction the UAW functioned superbly as a bread-and-butter union. Sufficiently sensitive and practical to know that most workers expected the union to produce a rising standard of living and judged the leadership by its ability to do so, Reuther never ignored or treated with condescension the material needs of those he represented. The gains of the auto workers were, of course, predicated on a prosperous industry and a union monopoly of the labor that went into American consumers' cars—conditions that, by and large, prevailed during Reuther's lifetime. Sympathetic to the members' demands for the material means to a more secure, fulfilling life, he nevertheless did not lose sight of the goals of social and economic justice for all citizens—goals that transcended the limits of business unionism.

IX

Labor United

OWING TO A COMPLICATED COMBINATION OF CAUSES, the labor movement lost much of its progressive momentum in the postwar era. The principal change was the disappearance of the depression-bred sense of the urgent need for social and economic reform; with the return of prosperity came the acceptance of a generally satisfactory status quo. Other factors were the defensive posture adopted in response to political attacks on labor, and the losses of energy and idealism stemming from labor's internal divisions. With few exceptions the CIO unions showed less interest in reform; their concerns by and large became almost indistinguishable from those of the AFL's business unionism. The leadership seemed tired, lacking commitment to principle. "The real sickness," wrote Daniel Bell, *Fortune*'s labor editor, in June 1953, "lies in the decline of unionism as a moral vocation. . . . Where there has not been outright spoliation, one finds among union leaders an appalling arrogance and high-handedness in their relation to the rank and file, which derives from the corruption of power." Reuther, Bell believed, was the one clear exception to these dismal generalizations—the only prominent figure who saw himself as the leader of a crusade.

Furthermore, unions had apparently reached boundaries to their growth. Approximately 25 percent of the civilian labor force was organized. Between 1945 and 1960 the numbers rose from 13 to 18 million, but the proportion remained the same. Most of the workers who were relatively easy to reach, the blue-collar manual workers of the Northeast and Midwest, were organized. Those remaining were white-collar workers, agricultural laborers, technicians, or professionals—all traditionally resistant to unionization—or blue-collar workers in areas hostile to unions, such as the South.

A comeback could begin with the unification of the federations. The issue that had originated their division, the refusal of the AFL to accept industrial organizations, was long since settled. The CIO industrial unions were permanently established; and several large AFL affiliates, such as the teamsters, machinists, and ladies' garment workers, were primarily industrial in nature. Nor were there significant differences in structure between the two federations, since both rested on the principle of the autonomy of the international unions, which alone could call strikes and engage in collective bargaining.

A heritage of bitter rivalry would have to be overcome, however. In the late 1930s the AFL had tried to destroy the CIO, accusing its officials of disloyalty and seeking changes in the Wagner Act and the NLRB that would favor its affiliates. President Roosevelt hoped to bring the two sides together before his 1940 campaign, but the negotiations collapsed because of conditions imposed by John L. Lewis. During the war the two federations cooperated on government advisory boards, but only under pressure, and quarreled over the organization of war workers.

Still, the liabilities of dual unionism were demonstrated almost daily. The job of organizing workers was difficult enough without adding interunion rivalry. To divide in the face of the opposition was to betray the interests of the workers. Several major organizing drives planned for the postwar years, especially a massive and badly needed CIO campaign in the South, bogged down. The passage of the Taft-Hartley Act in 1947 demonstrated the divided labor movement's political weakness. Some of these liabilities might be corrected by greater cooperation.

The deaths of Phillip Murray and William Green in 1952 cleared the way for new leaders with little personal investment in division. Reuther neither dominated CIO policy as Murray had, nor was he interested in maintaining the CIO as a separate organization. In the AFL the succession of George Meany went smoothly. He had served a long apprenticeship as secretary-treasurer and was on excellent terms with the members of the AFL council.

Meany and Reuther had very different experiences in the labor movement, and the future was to reveal differences of other kinds. Reuther's power was solidly based on his rise to the presidency of a large industrial union and his success in collective bargaining. Within the CIO he was something of an outsider, who had never been on close terms with Lewis or Murray. Meany, whose father was a local union official, was above everything else an insider. Although he had completed a plumber's apprenticeship in New York City and worked for a short time at the trade, he soon took office as business agent of a plumbers' local, then became secretary of the New York Building Trades Council, and later president of the New York State Federation of Labor. Since 1939 he had been the AFL's secretary-treasurer; he built his career on handling interunion disputes and on legislative lobbying. Lacking experience in collective bargaining or in administering a union, he boasted that he had never called or even participated in a strike.

Some limited cooperative experiments had already occurred. In 1952 the two federations had concluded a successful joint effort to secure greater labor representation on government boards involved in economic mobilization during the Korean War. Meany scuttled the committee when it appeared that it might go beyond that limited goal to consider unity, prompting Reuther to remark that, "this was the first time in the history of matrimony that divorce proceedings had been instituted because the marriage was too successful." Both Meany and Reuther, however, announced in favor of unity shortly after their elections. Reuther's support was conditioned on AFL progress in disciplining and, if necessary, expelling corrupt or gangster-ridden unions. He also insisted that a united federation must commit itself to eliminating racial discrimination within the movement.

In April 1953 a joint AFL-CIO unity committee met to tackle the problem of interunion raiding of members. The success of a no-raiding pact worked out in 1949 between the UAW and the International Association of Machinists of the AFL was encouraging. Meany and Reuther drafted a no-raiding agreement and secured its approval by the AFL and the CIO, although it was binding only on unions that signed it. The refusal of some of the major unions to accept the pact delayed its implementation; but by June 1954, 65 out of 110 AFL unions and 29 out of 32 CIO organizations had signed.

Among the powerful organizations that refused to sign were the carpenters and teamsters in the AFL and the steelworkers in the CIO, its largest affiliate at that time. President David J. McDonald, eager to take a line independent of Reuther, unexpectedly came out in favor of organic unity, not mere merger, of the two organizations. This aroused the enigmatic John L. Lewis, whose intentions, though not entirely clear, seemed to center on a new, unified organization in which he would play the leading role. Lewis, who had returned to the AFL with the coal miners in 1942 and then pulled out again in 1947, was distrusted by everyone. He encouraged McDonald to leave the CIO with savage, if ungrammatical, ridicule of Reuther. "You are unfortunate," he wrote, "in your affiliation with a federated group, dominated by intellectual inebriates and in frantic pursuit of butterflies of their delusions." However amusing Lewis's thrusts might be, McDonald realized that the steelworkers would never countenance a split with the CIO. Perhaps, too, Reuther and Meany felt some pressure from Lewis's rekindled ambitions. In October 1954 the AFL-CIO Joint Unity Committee decided "to create a single trade union center in America through the process of merger which will preserve the integrity of each affiliated national and international union."

Reuther's main reservation about unity stemmed from the presence of gangsters in some AFL unions. He insisted that known racketeers be thrown out before he could join. A particularly bad situation existed in the New York City locals of the International Longshoremen's Association, where a fight over corruption was raging at the very time unification was under discussion. Yielding to pressure from David Dubinsky and others, Meany intervened, but with little success. Reuther suspected that other AFL unions, including the teamsters, had criminal connections; later investigations proved him right.

There were other reasons for concern. Some of the UAW's officers feared that merger would turn the labor movement in a more conservative direction. The reform spirit of the CIO would be further diluted when labor policy had to clear an executive council of craft unionists under Meany's control. The AFL, larger by almost 3 million members than the CIO, would dominate the new federation no matter how hard Reuther and other progressive unionists pushed liberal causes. Furthermore, merger would add another layer of officialdom to the labor bureaucracy. Later events revealed the merit of these cogent criticisms.

Still, a strong case could be made for unity. A united labor movement could put together new organizational drives and would have more clout in political and legislative forums. To guard against AFL conservatism, Reuther counted on becoming the new organization's president before many years passed. Although he was content not to challenge Meany now, he expected him—at age sixty more than ten years Reuther's senior—to retire at a normal age and open the way for Reuther's succession.

The final negotiations took place in a luxury hotel in Miami Beach, a congenial and familiar setting for the AFL leaders but a discomfiting one for Reuther. On February 9, 1955, Meany and Reuther announced that full agreement had been reached. In the new AFL-CIO the affiliated unions' independence and integrity were guaranteed, and each retained its existing jurisdiction. Where jurisdictions overlapped, merger would be encouraged but not forced. The no-raiding agreement would be maintained on a voluntary basis and, along with the separate departments of the AFL, a new Industrial Union Department was established with Reuther as director, giving industrial unionism an equal place within the organization.

The program to which the two leaders pledged themselves reflected Reuther's ideas. The federation itself would become active in organizing the unorganized, a task Meany had believed should be left to the affiliates; it would launch a campaign against racketeering, guarantee equal treatment and the benefits of organization to workers regardless of race, and protect the trade union movement from "the undermining efforts of the Communist agencies and all others who are opposed to the basic principles of our democracy and of free and democratic unionism." Unofficially Reuther believed that a merged labor movement had to tackle the most difficult challenge of all: it had to "unionize the organized." The decline in the movement's morale and its loss of vigor were delicate subjects for labor leaders to discuss, but Reuther realized that something had to be done. Memories of the struggles of the 1930s were fading. Millions of new members had entered labor organizations with little or no recollection of preunion working conditions and wages or of the sacrifice and determination that had been required to create and nurture the unions. Since they took the achievements of the past for granted, the consciousness of these workers had to be raised.

There was never any question that Meany would become president of the AFL-CIO. Reuther disclaimed interest in the post. As he told a CIO convention just before the merger, "We don't care who leads the new labor movement providing it can be put together solidly and provided it is for the purpose of advancing the basic working interests of the American working groups." The new organization required full-time attention, but Reuther realized it would be foolish to exchange the presidency of the UAW for that of the AFL-CIO. Besides, Meany, with no position outside the federation, had nothing else to do. The CIO accepted another AFL stalwart, William Schnitzler, as secretary-treasurer. Reuther became vice-president and director of the Industrial Union Department.

Meany and Reuther jointly wielding a giant gavel opened the first convention of the new organization in December 1955. Its 15 million members made it the largest labor organization in American history. Although it had been expected that only CIO unions would enter the Industrial Union Department, several AFL unions—including the teamsters, who apparently plotted its takeover—asked to join. Many stepped in to limit their representation to the proportion of their membership that was industrial in character, preserving CIO control. The department nevertheless initially numbered over 7 million, nearly half the organization's membership, with an annual dues income of $1.7 million. Under Reuther it soon became the most active of the AFL-CIO's five departments. In his first speech to the convention Reuther called for a massive organizing drive, pledged $1.5 million to it, and set an ambitious goal of doubling the membership to 30 million in the next decade.

These high hopes were not fulfilled. A few unions, notably the teamsters, grew substantially, but the teamsters were later expelled from the AFL-CIO. The organizing campaigns conducted by the federation and by most of the affiliated member unions accomplished little. In the 1960s another surge in organizing occurred, mostly involving white-collar workers such as teachers and government employees; but many of their unions were outside the AFL-CIO. In addition, the blue-collar segment of the work force continued to shrink as a proportion of the total. Likewise, the number of jobs diminished in the older industrialized and unionized regions of the country. By 1964 AFL-CIO membership, far from doubling, had dropped to 13.5 million; although the expulsion of the teamsters accounted for most of the loss, membership losses by industrial unions were responsible for the rest. Within only a few years, many in labor became deeply discouraged over the prospects.

More progress was made toward eliminating corruption. In 1956 the authority of the AFL-CIO's Committee on Ethical Practices was enlarged, and a code of ethical practices for union officials was adopted. In an important departure from the principle of union autonomy, the federation won the right to expel affiliates whose officers were corrupt. These self-policing efforts failed to avert the storm.

Early in 1957 the Senate established a special committee under the chairmanship of Senator John McClellan, Democrat of Arkansas, to investigate "criminal or other improper practices or activities . . . in the field of labor-management relations." Although most labor leaders opposed the investigation as an attempt to smear honest labor organizations, Reuther took the position that corruption should be exposed by whatever means were necessary. The righteous had nothing to fear and everything to gain if wrongdoers were driven out. He urged that equal attention be given to corruption within management. As he told the committee, "Go after the crooks in the labor movement, but go after the crooks in management's side of the problem. When you find a crooked labor leader who took a bribe from a crooked employer, put them both in jail for about fifteen years and give them plenty of time to talk it over between themselves." The committee declined to follow Reuther's advice.

The McClellan committee's hearings concentrated on the teamsters' union, particularly the activities of its president, Dave Beck, and other officers. Strongly supported by Reuther, Meany engineered the removal of Beck from the AFL-CIO council; and, after James R. Hoffa had succeeded Beck as president, the teamsters and two other unions were expelled. The expulsion of the teamsters was a brave move since none of the union's officials at that time had been convicted, although Beck had taken the Fifth Amendment before the McClellan committee over ninety times.

Only one charge of corruption was lodged against a UAW official, vice-president Richard Gosser. With an affluent life-style that was out of place in the austere upper reaches of the UAW,

Gosser had already aroused Reuther's suspicions. An investigation by the board as far back as 1950 disclosed no wrongdoing, but Reuther had accepted that result with private reservations. In 1959 the McClellan committee investigated Gosser's affairs, which, it concluded (with considerable exaggeration), revealed a pattern of "kickbacks, terrorism, collusion with gamblers, conflicts of interest, destruction of records, and evasive tactics" comparable to Hoffa's irregularities. Reuther, sensing politics behind the inquiry, maintained that Gosser should be presumed innocent until he was tried, but eased him out of power and responsibility in the UAW, giving ill health as the reason. Although most of the charges against him were never proved, in 1963 Gosser was convicted of income tax fraud and sentenced to jail.

No charges were ever brought against Reuther, but he figured in a well-publicized side excursion of the McClellan committee. Senator Barry Goldwater and two other Republican members of the committee insisted on an investigation of the long, bitter strike of a UAW local against the Kohler Company of Sheboygan, Wisconsin, a manufacturer of bathroom fixtures. The UAW had won a representation election, but contract negotiations broke down. Mass picketing shut down the plant for fifty-four days until the company, with the help of an injunction, reopened with scab labor. Beatings of nonstrikers by two members of a Detroit UAW local were the focus of the committee's investigation. The two men testified that the local paid them to go to Wisconsin and support the strike but gave them no instructions. One got into a fight in a bar with a nonstriking Kohler worker for which he served thirteen months on an assault conviction. While he was in jail, the UAW helped support his family and paid for his lawyer. The other attacked a nonstriker who was working in a service station and his father, knocking both unconscious. A warrant was issued for his arrest; but he had returned to Michigan, and Governor G. Mennen Williams refused extradition without assurances of a fair trial. In his testimony, Reuther deplored the beatings and conceded that the Detroit local was at fault in failing to control its agents. There was no evidence that UAW officers had ordered the attacks, however. Reuther argued that the Michigan suspect should be extradited to Wisconsin when the authorities there agreed to a change of venue. Eventually the assailant was tried and served eighteen months in prison.

Reuther often seized the initiative during his questioning by the committee, particularly in a series of encounters with Senator Goldwater. He brought up a television statement of Goldwater's in which the senator had said that Kohler had a "right not to have a union if he can win a strike." Reuther lectured him on the law, pointing out that "only the employees under the law of these United States can make a decision whether they want a union and which union. An employer cannot make that decision without violating the law." "I would like to know," he continued, "whether you think under the Taft-Hartley law a company can decide not to have a union and destroy that union? I maintain they can't." Lamely Goldwater changed the subject: "I will tell you what, someday you and I are going to get together and lock horns." He then took refuge in the reminder that the witnesses were not supposed to ask the questions.

The legislative result of the hearings was the Landrum-Griffin Act of 1959, passed over the objections of labor. The law included an unexceptionable statement of members' rights and several provisions to guarantee democratic procedures in unions and to secure their funds from the grasp of avaricious officials. Other provisions of the law, however, had nothing to do with the disclosures of the McClellan committee but represented a further weakening of the legal status of organized labor. The Taft-Hartley ban on secondary boycotts was broadened, picketing rights were limited where a rival union was recognized, and the operations and jurisdiction of the NLRB were cut back in favor of giving the states more authority in labor-management relations. This last provision was probably the most important since it made organizing work even more difficult in states with hostile "right-to-work" laws.

Before the McClellan committee hearings began, the UAW in 1957 had launched an experiment, the establishment of a Public Review Board to protect the members' rights in a necessarily large and powerful organization. The usual procedure—still in effect in most unions—for a member who had a grievance against the union or who had been found guilty by trial of a violation of the union's constitution, was to appeal to the executive board for review, with a final appeal to the union's convention. On the assumption that the convention could be controlled by the union's officers, the Public Review Board was set up to provide an alternative disposition of the appeal. Its membership consisted of seven prominent "impartial persons of good repute" from outside the union. Clergymen, judges, and university professors have been favored. The board's hearings were public, its expenses paid without question by the UAW, and appellants entitled to counsel. Since its founding, the Public Review Board has not hesitated to reverse the executive board, far more often than the executive board has been reversed by conventions.

Unity and understanding among the world's free auto workers assumed greater significance with the internationalization of car manufacturing. Except for low-volume, high-cost sports and luxury models, few foreign-built cars had been sold in the United States. As the German and later the Japanese economies recovered from the ravages of war, however, their manufacturers began to export inexpensive cars to the United States. American manufacturers, in response to growth in overseas markets, expanded their foreign manufacturing capability. The extension of free trade encouraged manufacturers to locate new facilities to take advantage of low labor and materials costs, producing parts and cars wherever that could be done most cheaply and shipping them elsewhere for sale.

Reuther quickly recognized the potential impact of these changes on the jobs and living standards of American workers. "The day of the purely U.S. auto corporation is gone forever," he said. "Profits know no patriotism. . . . Technologies are the same and corporate policies are uniform, yet the workers are divided by national differences in social policies and in trade union custom and development. This is a division we must bridge." As early as 1956 he proposed the establishment of a world auto workers' council for Ford and GM workers to serve as a clearinghouse for information on wage rates, working conditions, and collective bargaining objectives in plants around the world. Ultimately the council would formulate bargaining demands. For the UAW it was crucial that foreign workers move toward wage parity with their American counterparts.

Reuther realized that differences of communication, living standards, and political and cultural values impeded the establishment of an effective council. Nevertheless, he preferred to aim for common standards and free trade instead of sealing off the United States market through protectionist legislation. Not until 1962 was the first world conference of auto workers held, and the first world auto council was established only in 1966. Whether such efforts would ever result in multinational unions bargaining with multinational corporations was doubtful. The problems became more difficult as rising fuel prices and inflation shifted demand toward smaller, more efficient vehicles. With capital needs for model development and plant investments becoming heavier, manufacturers set out to reduce costs. Whatever the outcome, Reuther and the UAW were among the first unionists to recognize the problems of the internationalization of the auto labor market and to work toward solutions that would recognize common interests.

Reuther's concern about worldwide working conditions and international relations often took him abroad for meetings and speaking engagements. His articulate advocacy of liberalism in labor and politics established common bonds with European trade unionists and democratic socialist politicians who shared this tradition. In fact, he often received a heartier welcome from European counterparts than from his American colleagues. At a meeting of the Trade Union Congress in Great Britain in 1957, he moved a large audience of union leaders with a stirring account of the gains American workers had won. "No overseas visitor in living memory," wrote a London reporter, "has made such an immense impact by his personality and tempestuous oratory."

Almost from the time of the AFL-CIO merger, Meany and Reuther differed over issues of foreign policy. Meany rigidly divided the world between supporters and opponents of communism. He scorned neutralists who tried to protect their nations and reduce tensions by allying with neither of the two superpowers, the United States and the USSR. Soon after he became AFL-CIO president, Meany denounced Prime Minister Nehru of India and Marshal Tito of Yugoslavia (the latter had broken decisively with the USSR in 1948), as "aides and allies of Communism in fact and in effect if not in diplomatic verbiage." Reuther, however, recognized and respected positions on world affairs that differed from those taken by the United States. Though unswerving in opposing Communist totalitarianism and Soviet self-aggrandizement, he did not believe that undeviating allegiance to American objectives was the sole test of virtue. Furthermore, he considered it his duty to point out his differences with Meany. The issues were too important to permit anyone to conclude that Meany expressed the view of the whole labor movement. Shortly after Meany's criticism of Nehru, Reuther visited India. He described Nehru as "truly one of the great statesmen of the world" and criticized United States policy in Asia for placing "undue emphasis upon military power, military pacts, and military alliances. This . . . has, in my opinion, tended to trade reliable democratic friends for doubtful military allies." Reuther's remarks, by showing the Indian government and people that an influential American labor leader recognized and appreciated their commitment to democracy, independence, and neutrality, were, as an Indian newspaper wrote, "a most welcome whiff of fresh air."

To give substance to his belief that peace depended on a vast and continuing sharing of resources, skills, and wealth, Reuther proposed that the United States pledge 2 percent of its gross national product for a period of twenty-five years to a United Nations–administered fund to assist less developed nations in improving their standards of living, health, and education. The USSR and other industrialized nations would be challenged to do the same, starting an era of peaceful competitive coexistence. Reuther also proposed the establishment of a United Nations task force of skilled young Americans and others to provide technical and educational assistance. American economic aid, he believed, should "be made available to every free and independent nation without any political strings whatsoever," a formula that included unaligned nations like India but omitted those in the Communist bloc.

A significant clash between Reuther and Meany occurred over the question of meetings with the Soviet leaders Nikita Khrushchev and Anastas Mikoyan during their visits to the United States in 1959. Meany held that the USSR was the enemy of free unions: it had none of its own, it wiped them out wherever it could, and its claim to be the workers' state was fraudulent. He would not meet in any forum with Soviet leaders because to do so would endorse their state-controlled workers' organizations. When Mikoyan, the deputy premier of the USSR, arrived in the United States he announced that he would like to visit the Washington headquarters of the AFL-CIO. Meany, however, locked the doors of the federation's palatial building, forcing the Soviet official to peer through its massive windows to catch a glimpse of the leaders of the American working class going about their business. Reuther and three other AFL-CIO vice-presidents invited Mikoyan to lunch; Meany declined an invitation, however, curtly dismissing those who "feel that they can meet the Soviet challenge at the conference table." Reuther's position was that Soviet leaders should be confronted directly by representatives of American workers so that they could know the full measure of the workers' objections to their policies.

The luncheon with Mikoyan was only a warm-up for a dinner with Khrushchev in San Francisco in September 1959. Meany once again refused to participate and pushed a resolution through the AFL-CIO council attacking the Soviet system when the Soviet leader arrived in the United States. The dinner, attended by six labor leaders, the Russians, and some aides and interpreters, lasted five hours. Interludes of calm discussion alternated with many sharp exchanges.

Khrushchev: "The United States exploits the wealth of other countries, underdeveloped countries, for profits. . . . We do not exploit any country—we only engage in trade."

Reuther: "You exploit the workers of East Germany."

Khrushchev: "Where did you dream that up?"

Reuther: "If you don't exploit them, why should three million of them cross the border into West Germany?"

Khrushchev: "You are feverish. . . . "

Reuther: "Do you have credentials to speak for the workers of the world?"

Khrushchev: "Do you have credentials to poke your nose into East Germany?"

Reuther questioned Khrushchev closely about the lack of independence of Soviet unions, a subject of great interest to the absent Meany. Khrushchev finally shouted. "Why poke your nose into our business?" "Freedom," Reuther replied, "is everybody's business." When he tried to continue, a red-faced Khrushchev shouted. "We call what you represent—capitalist lackeys!" One of the few topics on which the two moralists agreed was that the movie *Can Can*, which Khrushchev had seen in production in Hollywood and which he crudely burlesqued for the Americans, was a vulgar film, although the Soviet premier insisted that capitalism was responsible for its salaciousness.

After Khrushchev returned to the USSR, he struck a last blow through the press in a story claiming that Reuther had married while in the USSR, fathered a child, and then abandoned his family. The undocumented charges were denied by Reuther and dismissed by Americans as a reprisal for the embarrassment Khrushchev had suffered. The *Detroit News*, which ordinarily showed little sympathy for Reuther, commented: "The Russians, who have a talent for abuse that approaches genius, have surpassed themselves in their vilification of Walter P. Reuther. The UAW president has been assaulted with a variety of unkind nouns and adjectives in his own country, but it took Moscow to decide that he is a bigamist." Although Khrushchev's clownish behavior led some Americans to dismiss the whole episode, the Soviet premier clearly perceived the philosophical gulf that separated the Soviet system from Reuther's belief in free unions within a democracy. In Vienna in 1961, a grim Khrushchev told President John F. Kennedy, "We hung the likes of Reuther in Russia in 1917."

As the 1960 election approached, Reuther became the most active in national politics of all labor leaders. After eight years of a middle-of-the-road administration, with the controversial Richard Nixon the likely Republican presidential nominee, the political pendulum was due for a swing to the Democrats and a liberal government. John F. Kennedy, Hubert H. Humphrey, Adlai E. Stevenson, Stuart Symington, and Lyndon B. Johnson were the candidates for the Democratic nomination—all except Johnson acceptable to the UAW and Reuther. Reuther remained officially neutral and the UAW made no preconvention endorsement; but behind the scenes he was involved. In the primaries, Kennedy and Humphrey emerged as the leading contenders, with Johnson and Stevenson in the background. Although Humphrey had strong claims on both labor and the civil rights movement, Reuther was more attracted to Kennedy. As a member of the McClellan committee, the Massachusetts senator had provided helpful support during its hearings; and, more important, it appeared that he could mount a stronger campaign against Nixon. Reuther's friend Eleanor Roosevelt begged him not to foreclose the possibility of supporting Stevenson, but Reuther feared that a weakening of Kennedy would be to Johnson's advantage.

At the convention a boomlet for Stevenson collapsed. Kennedy won on the first ballot with the support of Reuther and the forty UAW delegates, more than from any other union. The hottest issue was the vice-presidential nomination, with Reuther favoring Humphrey, who, however, was not interested. Kennedy stunned Reuther and most liberals by offering the place to Johnson. Although he had many reservations about Johnson's record, Reuther, at Kennedy's request, stepped in to head off a revolt in the Michigan delegation against the nomination, and dissuaded George Meany from pushing a critical resolution through the AFL-CIO council. As it turned out, Johnson's presence on the ticket helped give Kennedy his narrow margin of victory; after Johnson succeeded Kennedy in 1963, his liberal accomplishments at home surpassed those of any president since FDR.

The UAW threw itself into the campaign. Roy Reuther, a wheelhorse in the union's political activities, became codirector of the Democratic party's voter registration committee, a key to ensuring a large Democratic turnout. Nixon, believing he could turn the visibility of the UAW and the Reuthers to his own account, denounced Walter as a "labor leader turned radical politician" and warned the nation that with Kennedy in the White House Reuther would "have a lot to do with calling the tune." In fact, Reuther exercised no extraordinary influence. On most matters of interest to the labor movement, Kennedy followed the advice of George Meany over that of Reuther whenever there was a conflict. In the extremely close election, Kennedy carried Michigan, Illinois, Missouri, New York, and Delaware, states with large numbers of UAW members, but lost Ohio, Indiana, and Wisconsin, which also had many auto unionists.

Reuther approved Kennedy's domestic program, especially measures that promised to revive a flagging economy, like the Manpower Development Act, which for the first time began job retraining for displaced workers. He recognized, however, that the president was hampered by insufficient congressional support. As he wrote Eleanor Roosevelt, with whom he regularly corresponded and visited, "Our real problem is going to be on the legislative front." Once again a liberal president, confronting the southern Democrat–Republican coalition, won few victories.

The results of the 1962 congressional elections, in which the UAW was especially active, were encouraging, however. In both houses the liberal element gained strength.

For Reuther—"the one white labor leader of national stature who was close to both the NAACP and Martin Luther King," in the words of two historians of civil rights—the great public event of the Kennedy years was King's massive march on Washington in August 1963. A long-time member of the NAACP board of directors and a champion of racial justice, Reuther had already responded to several appeals from Attorney-General Robert Kennedy for help in civil rights causes—supplying, for example, $160,000 in UAW funds as bail for some of King's followers held in a Birmingham jail. As plans for a civil rights demonstration in Washington went forward, Reuther found himself caught between King and the Kennedy administration, which feared that a large demonstration might be an occasion for violence. Furthermore, an all-black demonstration would upset southern congressmen whose acquiescence in civil rights legislation was essential for passage. At the request of government officials, Reuther helped mobilize and add to the march some sympathetic white elements, including many UAW members, other labor groups, and representatives of religious organizations. The result was the most impressive public demonstration of interracial backing for civil rights in the nation's history. It provided the forum for King's stirring "I Have a Dream" speech and led to the passage of the civil rights acts of 1964 and 1965.

Reuther tried to obtain Meany's cooperation and the official support of the AFL-CIO for the Washington march, but Meany—who preferred to approach power through the back corridors rather than the streets—refused. After turning down Reuther's request for an endorsement and money, the AFL-CIO council passed a resolution recognizing the right of affiliated unions and their members to participate in the march and to support it financially. An irritated Reuther snapped, "That resolution is so anemic it will need a transfusion to get to the mimeograph machine," but it was the best he could get. The march was supported with funds and members by the UAW and several other CIO unions, with Reuther among the participants.

Reuther was especially happy with some aspects of Kennedy's foreign policy. Without eschewing military aid to threatened nations, the president strove to balance it with economic, technical, scientific, and educational assistance. Reuther recognized the necessity of maintaining American military strength, but in prescribing assistance for other countries he strongly emphasized the superiority of nonmilitary aid. He repeatedly warned against using weapons to prop up reactionary regimes whose sole claim to United States support was their anti-communist stance. He believed that building up the economies and societies of war-ravaged or poor nations with long-term projects and assistance could help to produce permanently strong and prosperous nations. Although Reuther generally favored the United Nations and other international agencies as the best channel for assistance, he had warmly supported such United States initiatives as the Marshall Plan and Truman's Point Four program of technical assistance.

One of the most exciting Kennedy proposals was that for a Peace Corps. The general idea of a voluntary assistance agency had been put forward for years; its roots lay in the medical and other services supplied under missionary auspices by earlier generations. As early as 1950 the UAW recommended creation by government of an overseas technical aid program. Reuther, whose sojourn in the USSR as a die maker set a personal precedent, developed a proposal to establish government-funded college scholarships. Young men who accepted them would, on graduation, have the option of serving abroad for three years in a civilian agency or for two years in the military. In a 1956 speech to an educational conference he stated the belief

that the more young Americans we send throughout the world as technical missionaries with slide rules, with medical kits, with textbooks, to fight Communism on a positive basis, the fewer young Americans we will need to send with guns and flamethrowers to fight Communism on the battlefields of the world. The kind of educational program I am thinking about would make it possible to enlist thousands of young Americans in the rewarding struggle to win the peace.

Toward the end of the decade a few politicians, including Congressman Henry Reuss and Senator Hubert Humphrey, adopted the idea and introduced bills for its implementation. In 1959 Victor Reuther endorsed a proposal in testimony before the Senate Foreign Relations Committee. With Reuther and others urging him on, Kennedy introduced his Peace Corps proposal in the campaign of 1960, although he quickly dropped the option of civilian or military service when Richard Nixon charged that the plan would create a haven for draft dodgers. With Kennedy's backing the Peace Corps elicited an enthusiastic response from idealistic youth, and its members earned the gratitude of nearly all of the nations that accepted them.

Reuther drew closer to the Democratic party in the Eisenhower and Kennedy years. By working closely with a liberal administration, Reuther could help strengthen its commitment to policies he believed essential, although it also meant associating himself with other policies and decisions that he could not entirely accept. Association with the Democrats was also a defensive political necessity. The revival of close, two-party competition, after the long Roosevelt era of one-party domination, curtailed labor's political independence. With the gradual erosion of the Roosevelt political coalition, the two major parties were in balance only as long as labor remained firmly within the Democratic camp. If labor held back, the balance would tip toward the Republicans, with hostile legislation as the likely result. While Kennedy was in the White House, the benefits of this strategy outweighed its disadvantages. Under his successor, Lyndon B. Johnson, however, the price went up.

The reunification of labor failed to accomplish much of what had been hoped. Although Reuther and Meany agreed on many trade union matters and were equally committed to an active, clean organization, disagreements over some policies and personality clashes had already appeared. Soon deeper fissures developed.

X

Uneasy Alliances

THE DECADE OF THE 1960S was one of opportunities that in the end were unrealized. Reuther's smoldering dispute with George Meany over the direction of labor exploded in 1968 in the UAW's withdrawal from the AFL-CIO. Although the presidency of Lyndon B. Johnson began with bright promises that were partly fulfilled, the Vietnam War ultimately shattered his political base and drove him from office. The assassinations of Robert F. Kennedy and of Martin Luther King in 1968, five years after John F. Kennedy's death, destroyed liberalism's most inspiring, steadfast spokesmen. For the American worker, times were generally prosperous, but the auto companies and ultimately the work force faced challenges posed by rising sales of imported cars and added costs for safety and pollution-control equipment. Employment at the Big Three rose from about 700,000 in 1961 to nearly 1,000,000 by 1966 and remained high for the rest of the decade. The composition of the work force, however, underwent a massive change as the generation that had built the UAW stepped down from jobs and union offices.

Reuther and Meany were at odds through most of the decade. Their association was never close, although on some issues their views were similar and at times they worked together effectively. At bottom, their disagreement stemmed from different conceptions of the purpose of unions, aggravated by conflicting personal values. Meany was a business unionist who stressed the workers' material interests. When asked what unions wanted, he repeated Samuel Gompers's famous reply to the same question:

"More!" The labor federation, he believed, should confine itself to the important but secondary roles of keeping the affiliated unions honest and representing the membership's common interests in legislative and political matters. Meany was an active politician who expected to be consulted on legislation and government appointments of importance to labor and deferred to as its spokesman on public questions. He made few efforts to direct public opinion, preferring to conduct the federation's political affairs through contacts and bargaining with the powerful.

To Reuther the union was a champion of reform as well as the instrument of the members' material interests. He believed a vital labor federation should reflect that enlarged conception. The federation should be an agency of public benefit, its leader a public figure who could express and forward aspirations for social justice. Unions should not confine themselves to a minor role; they could, he believed, be the future's creative shaping force. Under Meany's leadership, Reuther feared, labor was not only falling back from the vanguard of progress but was also in danger of dropping out of the liberal movement. Reuther wanted to restore unions to the place they had won among the forces for change in the great upheaval of the 1930s.

Different styles of life reflected differences in values. An advocate of business unionism, Meany drew a large salary plus a generous expense account and lived commensurately well. Though devoted to his job, he found time for other things. After a working day of ordinary length, he went home to a martini. Although he retained his Bronx accent, he acquired a gourmet's taste in food and wine; smoked expensive cigars; and enjoyed golf, once a sport of the wealthy. The annual AFL-CIO council's winter meeting, a lavish spectacle, was always held in luxurious quarters, usually a Miami Beach oceanfront hotel. Meetings and appointments occupied part of the day; but there was plenty of time left over to spend at night clubs, lounging around the swimming pool, or at the race track. Meany loved gin rummy, and his union pals always carried a deck of cards. One joke in labor circles was that he had won Jay Lovestone—the AFL-CIO's anticommunist foreign policy advisor and Reuther's one-time UAW adversary—from David Dubinsky in a card game.

Reuther considered Meany's *dolce vita* both a cause and a symbol of the labor movement's decline. Leaders should share the workers' standard of living. If they embraced materialism and affluence, envy and cynicism would spread in the ranks, undermining the idealism and solidarity Reuther believed were the future's best hope. He was outraged that AFL-CIO council meetings were held in Florida, remote from the cold factory cities in which the workers whose dues paid the bills remained at their jobs. These feelings, openly expressed, were ridiculed and resented by other labor chieftains. During the Miami meetings that concluded the merger agreement, Reuther had refused to use a large hotel suite reserved for him, insisting on moving to smaller quarters. James Carey, president of the International Union of Electrical Workers and a Reuther ally, occupied the vacated suite and made fun of his friend's scruples, telling inquiring newsmen that Reuther could be found down the hall in the linen closet, squeezing his own orange juice.

Reuther's personal idealism, crystallized into character, dictated his reaction. He had patterned his behavior on the model of an ideal workman—one who was master of a trade and of himself, for whom a job well done was life's greatest satisfaction. His trade was that of a union leader. It required total devotion and resistance to any temptations that might impair his performance. Reuther worked hard and took few vacations, although, with an eye to retirement, he had purchased a small home near Fort Myers, Florida. With an annual salary of $31,000 when he died in 1970 (Meany then received over $90,000), he was among the lowest-paid presidents of major unions, and he lived frugally. He had little interest in food and none in drink. His UAW expense account was relatively small and scrupulously accounted for. He took the generous expense account the AFL-CIO provided those attending its council meetings but turned it over to the UAW, paying his expenses out of the smaller amount provided by his union. The fees he received for speeches went to a foundation that provided college scholarships for workers' children. Even his recreation reflected the craftsman's tastes and habits. He favored the solitude and the patient, precise skills of cabinetmaking and fishing, with now and then a game of tennis—not the febrile excitements (as he judged them) of horse races and card games. To Reuther the indulgences of the Meany crowd were not only inappropriate, they were unnatural.

Interwoven in the dispute between Meany and Reuther were conflicting ambitions. Each aspired to be the voice of the labor movement, and each believed he had earned the right. Reuther was tried and proven in all dimensions of union leadership: strikes, negotiations, and setting out an enlightened position on public issues. Meany's experience, confined to state and national labor bureaucracies, struck Reuther as too narrow. The AFL-CIO president had, however, carefully cultivated the support of the organization's council members; and he met their expectations of a federation president. Undoubtedly Reuther expected Meany, who was thirteen years his senior and turned sixty-five in 1959, to retire. He misread the man. Meany lived for his position and clung to it almost until the day of his death in 1980 at the age of eighty-five, ten years after the accident that took Reuther's life.

The two men's differences in outlook surfaced in encounters on a series of issues. The first was the question of organizing the unorganized. Reuther had set as the federation's goal a doubling of its membership to 30 million. As the work force expanded, the labor movement had to grow merely to hold its own. Not only were improvements for the unorganized at stake, but the presence of a mass of low-paid workers also undermined the standards of the unionized, a graver threat to the less skilled workers of the mass-production industries than to craft union members. Reuther insisted that the office of director of organization, the highest-paid post in the AFL-CIO that went to a CIO figure, go to a veteran UAW organizer, John Livingston.

Meany paid more than lip service to the goal of organization, but he did not favor a massive joint effort. Organizing campaigns, he believed, should be carried out by the affiliated unions. Reflecting the traditional view of the AFL, Meany disliked assessing union members to pay for campaigns among workers who would eventually join a different union, in most cases an industrial organization. This position ignored the fact that the stronger industrial unions, like the UAW, had fully organized their jurisdictions. Their resources in money and manpower could be most effectively tapped through the federation. Furthermore, in the segments of the economy in which the number of jobs was growing most rapidly, such as white-collar and service work, there were few strong unions. A centralized organizing campaign drawing on the entire federation made sense.

After several attempts to gain Meany's cooperation had failed, Reuther concentrated his efforts on organizing drives conducted by the Industrial Union Department, but a task that would have stretched the resources of the entire AFL-CIO to the limit was too much for a portion of it. By the end of the 1960s membership in unions had increased from 16 million at the time of the merger to 19 million, but had fallen from roughly one-third to one-fourth of the nonagricultural segment of the expanding work force. Even so, the most successful campaigns of the decade had been those of the expelled Teamsters' Union.

Although the overall result was disappointing, there were organizing drives that echoed the vitality and idealism of the 1930s. The most stirring was the effort of Cesar Chavez to bring the ill-paid laborers of California's fields and vineyards into the United Farm Workers. Walter, urged by Roy Reuther and Paul Schrade, UAW regional director on the West Coast, was the first union president to enlist in Chavez's cause. The UAW and the Industrial Union Department provided key financial aid and cooperated with liberal and religious groups in organizing support for a national boycott of nonunion grapes, a crucial part of Chavez's strategy. In December 1965, Reuther visited striking grape pickers in Delano and met Chavez. Declaring, "I haven't felt anything like this since the old days," he led a march of Chavez's followers, a delicate undertaking since Chavez's group was not then supported by the AFL-CIO, and the local police chief had threatened arrest. Later he conferred with the growers to urge their acceptance of the union and pledged a $5,000-a-month contribution to the strikers, half from the Industrial Union Department and half from the UAW. He impulsively added another $5,000 as a Christmas present. Chavez recalled Reuther's visit as "a very significant day" because of the financial and moral support it produced and the favorable national publicity it generated.

Reuther sought to expand Chavez's base of support. In 1966 he persuaded Senator Robert F. Kennedy, a member of the Senate's Migratory Labor Subcommittee, to attend hearings in California, where Kennedy gained firsthand information on the exploitation of agricultural workers, met Chavez, and became a political champion of the farm workers. Reuther had less success with Meany, whom he urged to go beyond the financial aid the AFL-CIO had finally extended by traveling to California to make an endorsement. Meany, with no appreciation of the importance of public demonstrations of support, refused. Earlier he had excluded Reuther from membership on an AFL-CIO committee set up to assist the farm workers, despite the fact that the original suggestion for the committee came from Reuther, the only member of the council who had visited the farm workers' headquarters and given them personal assistance.

Closely related to organizing was the issue of conflicting jurisdictional claims. Job rights had always been troublesome for labor federations, a situation now aggravated by declining numbers of jobs and union members in some fields of employment. The merger brought the question to the fore, since not all the unions had accepted the earlier no-raiding agreement. Craft workers in industrial plants were usually members of an industrial union. In auto factories, for example, the carpenters who built wooden forms and performed maintenance work belonged to the UAW. After the merger the carpenters' union laid claim to these jobs, and some other craft unions followed suit. In a few instances, industrial unions claimed jobs within their industries that had been organized by craft unions.

The AFL-CIO lacked an effective mechanism for resolving these conflicts. When Reuther took the initiative by warning that rival claims could split the federation, Meany set up a committee headed by A. J. Hayes, president of the Machinists' Union. The committee majority, including Hayes and Reuther, proposed binding outside arbitration of job rights disputes, a position at odds with the interests and traditions of the building trades. At a council session that lasted until 3:40 A.M., the issue was thrashed out. Meany proposed concessions to the craft unions, suggesting that arbitrators' rulings should be subject to council review and that no union should be compelled to accept them. Any union that refused could be penalized, however. This, he argued, would give him the leverage to resolve disputes prior to arbitration. Reuther was so upset that he wanted to walk out of the meeting—and presumably out of the federation—but the presidents of the other CIO unions refused to budge. After some minor concessions to Reuther, Meany won over the reluctant building trades' presidents to support of his compromise. Politically, Reuther's challenge had failed, but on the point at issue he obtained a settlement that ended threats to the integrity of industrial unions.

Reuther suffered other affronts, some unconscionably petty, as Meany exerted his presidential prerogatives. Meany omitted Reuther from an escort committee for President John F. Kennedy at an AFL-CIO convention, although Reuther was far better acquainted with the new president than any other labor leader and the UAW had poured resources into Kennedy's campaign. Meany later claimed the omission was an oversight, but few believed him. He blocked several appointments Reuther favored, including one of Reuther himself to the United States delegation to the United Nations. Adlai E. Stevenson, Kennedy's

U.N. ambassador, had requested that Reuther be named. Reuther himself was eager to serve and believed that American labor should be represented at the United Nations. Meany refused, however, and Kennedy would not proceed without his consent. Meany's avowed reason was that Reuther had not first cleared the appointment through him; but in view of their rivalry and conflicting views on foreign policy, more than protocol was involved. Since no one else was acceptable to Stevenson, no labor representative was appointed. Similarly, Meany blocked the appointment of Reuther's assistant Jack Conway as undersecretary of labor. Reuther had written to Kennedy recommending the appointment. Meany resented Reuther's direct approach and later claimed that a mere phone call to him would have cleared the way, but Reuther suspected that no one from the UAW would have been acceptable. In any event, Reuther believed he had earned the right to act independently of Meany. The AFL-CIO president had withheld full support from Kennedy in 1960, whereas the UAW had conducted the most active campaign of any of the nation's unions on his behalf.

Although opposed to the selection of Lyndon B. Johnson as the Democrats' vice-presidential candidate in 1960, Reuther established a harmonious relationship with him during the Kennedy administration and quickly rallied to him after Kennedy's assassination. Johnson called Reuther the day after the tragedy, as he called many of Kennedy's friends, to solicit support. Before the assassination, Congress had been moving toward passage of legislation that Reuther had long advocated. Now Johnson's political skills and the desire to fulfill the slain president's dreams were added to the momentum that was building up for new civil rights, antipoverty, extended Social Security benefits, and urban renewal laws. Before the 1964 election Reuther expressed the hope that the Republicans would make Senator Barry Goldwater their presidential candidate in order to give the voters a real choice and to move the parties toward a more clear-cut ideological division. He must have rejoiced when the Republicans, perhaps for the only time, followed his advice. With a Republican opponent who turned millions of independents and moderates into Democratic voters, Johnson won in a landslide, pulling in the largest liberal congressional majorities in a generation. From 1964 until 1966, when countercurrents flowing from the Vietnam War undermined the liberal consensus, the government produced the greatest flood of innovative legislation since the height of the New Deal, an achievement to which Reuther contributed as much as any private citizen.

Reuther played a major role in mobilizing opinion for the memorable campaign in behalf of civil rights, the era's most constructive and overdue reform. Although in 1960 he had urged the Democratic convention to extract a pledge from Johnson to support effective civil rights laws, Reuther's work with him on President Kennedy's Committee on Equal Employment Opportunity—which Johnson, as vice-president, chaired—assured him that the new president would be a strong proponent of equal rights. Testifying in 1963 before Congress, Reuther recommended new laws more sweeping than those proposed by Kennedy, including the use of federal registrars for voter registration of southern blacks, the device adopted in the Voting Rights Act of 1965. He was the only white labor representative among the ten leaders of the 1963 Washington civil rights demonstration. When marches in southern cities emerged as an effective method of mobilizing support, Reuther took his place in the ranks. In 1965 Walter and May Reuther went to Selma, Alabama, where Martin Luther King and hundreds of others were demonstrating for voting rights. There they joined in marches and led a UAW delegation of over 2,000 in a memorial tribute to the recently martyred Reverend James Reeb, actions that prompted many UAW locals to adopt resolutions of commendation and pride in their president's witness for equal rights. A few months later the Reuthers joined James H. Meredith in Jackson, Mississippi, for a similar civil rights march.

Like nearly everyone who came into Johnson's furious

orbit, Reuther was pressed into political service. At the Democratic convention in 1964, the all-white "regular" delegation from Mississippi was challenged by the Mississippi Freedom Democratic Party, an integrated but largely black group that truthfully contended that the regulars neither agreed with the national party's position on civil rights nor represented many of the state's citizens. Johnson, fearing that a walkout by southern whites would lead to loss of their states to Goldwater, wanted a compromise. His operatives first proposed to seat the regulars, allow the Freedom Democrats to appear on the floor but not vote, and pledge that rules changes would ensure representative delegations in the future. The Freedom Democrats, who wanted to seat both delegations and divide the votes between them, would not accept the Johnson proposal. Furthermore, they threatened to remove the struggle from the Credentials Committee to the convention floor, where many delegates from northern states would support them. Johnson instructed Hubert Humphrey to "get ahold of Walter Reuther and see if he can help you"—aware, no doubt, of Reuther's standing with blacks and of the fact that Joseph L. Rauh, Jr., an advisor to the Freedom Democrats, was an attorney and lobbyist for the UAW and Reuther's friend.

At first Reuther, involved in negotiations with General Motors, was reluctant to go on this errand; but Humphrey persuaded him to fly to Atlantic City. There he met with Johnson's advisors and the Freedom Democrats and produced a compromise that reflected the president's wishes but added two Freedom Democrats, Aaron Henry and Ed King, as voting delegates. The proposal split the Freedom Democrats. Some favored its acceptance but held that a representative of poor, black Mississippians, Fannie Lou Hamer, should be added. Others rejected it altogether. In the end, most of the regular Mississippi delegates walked out of the convention anyway because of the compromise's demand for loyalty to the party's platform plank on civil rights and its assurance of fair treatment in future delegate selection. In the election Goldwater carried

Mississippi and four other southern states, but Johnson so overwhelmed his Republican opponent elsewhere that these defections were neither needed nor missed.

Many expected that Reuther, with his commitments to civil rights and higher standards of living for ordinary people, would enthusiastically enlist in Johnson's war on poverty; but he was not an unquestioning soldier in the ranks. He looked on the Johnson plan as "a good beginning, but . . . only a beginning." The UAW gave $1.1 million, one of the campaign's largest sums from a private source, to establish the Citizens Crusade Against Poverty (CCAP) with Reuther as chairman. With Johnson's approval, the Crusade organized support among more than 125 liberal, labor, civil rights, and church organizations in behalf of antipoverty laws and appropriations; coordinated the antipoverty efforts of private agencies; conducted important inquiries into poverty-related problems such as the extent of hunger and malnutrition; and planned a program of massive proportions for training antipoverty workers. In April 1966, as antipoverty appropriations were pinched to fund escalation of the war in Vietnam, Reuther criticized Johnson before a Poor People's Poverty Convention in Washington. "It is a mistake," he chided, "to trim your sails before the fight." Poverty could not be abolished by doling out money "with an eye-dropper." An effective program, he argued, required sums at least as large as the billions going each year to Vietnam.

A major aim of CCAP was to back a controversial feature of Johnson's plan calling for involvement of the poor themselves in setting the goals and administering the program. Known as maximum feasible participation, this idea that the rank and file of the poor should have a say in what was done and participate directly in improving their condition paralleled union principles and practices but led to conflicts with mayors and other local politicians who wished to control disbursement of funds and jobs. The Citizens Crusade, with Ford Foundation funds, trained more than a thousand community workers in organizing and administrative techniques.

A confrontation resulted from the decision of Sargent Shriver, head of the government's major antipoverty agency, the Office of Economic Opportunity, to discontinue funding the Child Development Group of Mississippi. The Group, which operated a Head Start program for preschoolers serving more than 12,000 children and used the poor in administrative posts, was the nation's largest and one of the most effective programs for poor blacks. The Johnson administration, Reuther charged, bowed to pressure from Mississippi politicians "more interested in preserving the status quo in Mississippi than they are in helping disadvantaged children." Although most of the funds were restored in this instance, Reuther feared the war on poverty was falling victim to the Vietnam adventure and the politicians' hostility.

Johnson sought Reuther's advice on many issues. He was frequently at the White House; and a stream of telegrams, letters, reports, and resolutions—on housing and urban development, health care, school aid, consumer protection, civil rights, conservation and beautification, inflation, car prices, the impact of automation, international trade, nuclear nonproliferation, and a host of other matters—flowed from UAW headquarters to Washington. As the Johnson administration dealt with long-neglected domestic problems, Reuther felt the UAW's commitments to reform and the Democratic party were paying off.

Success came at a heavy price, however. As Johnson racked up the greatest domestic gains since the New Deal, he took hostages among the liberals. Critics of his Vietnam policy risked destroying the coalition that produced reform at home. Ironically, and tragically, Reuther, who had always believed that social justice could be achieved only through peaceful reconstruction and aid, bound himself to a president who placed his faith in war. His commitment to Johnson also restrained Reuther in his criticisms of Meany, a warlord whose support of a tough policy of military escalation was nearly automatic. Opposing Meany involved the risk of isolating Reuther from Johnson. For the duration of the president's term, Reuther exerted whatever pressure he could on both Johnson and Meany for a peaceful settlement and a deemphasis on war—but within narrow limits designed to avoid a break with the president.

In March 1965, when Johnson escalated the war with air attacks on North Vietnam and the commitment of United States troops to the ground war in South Vietnam, the UAW board unanimously adopted a position statement rejecting the two "unacceptable alternatives"—withdrawal of American forces from Vietnam and greater reliance on military means. Though refraining from direct criticism of Johnson, the statement pointed out the dangers of escalation and argued for an un-specified political solution worked out through negotiations, including use of an international, preferably UN, peacekeeping force. In transmitting the resolution to Congress, Reuther spoke of the "increasing disquiet among our own members over the implications of our government's policy." This low-keyed acknowledgment of dissent within the UAW was amplified in early May when Emil Mazey, its secretary-treasurer, attacked the South Vietnamese government for oppressing its people and charged that Johnson was making a "serious mistake in es-calating the war." Reuther maintained that Mazey had every right to criticize as a private citizen as long as it was clear that his views did not represent those of the UAW.

In April 1965 Johnson defended his Vietnam policy in a speech at Johns Hopkins University. Although the bulk of his address depicted an aggressive North Vietnam invading its neighbor, and invoked the shades of Munich to condemn appeasement, Reuther latched on to the president's promise of economic aid and his willingness to enter into "unconditional negotiations"—a misleading phrase since Johnson always in-sisted that United States forces remain in Vietnam during talks. Nevertheless, in a later "redefinition" of its position, the UAW board stated its support for the "current administration policy of insuring against Communist military victory while holding forth the hand of unconditional negotiations."

The AFL-CIO confronted the question at its convention a few weeks later. Meany proposed a resolution endorsing only military action, but Reuther insisted that the administration's willingness to negotiate should also be approved. Threatened with a floor fight, which both Meany and Johnson wished to avoid, a compromise of sorts was fashioned that pledged "unstinting support" of "all measures the Administration might deem necessary to halt Communist aggression and secure a just and lasting peace," including negotiations. In press conference comments Reuther tried to weaken his association with the hard-line implications of the statement, saying that although it was "acceptable, it was not written the way I would have written it." He interpreted the statement as taking a "position that stands midpoint between two extreme[s]" of unilateral withdrawal and unlimited escalation.

On issues not involving Johnson administration policy, Reuther freely expressed his opposition to Meany's views. The first open, public disagreement between them in over three years occurred in June 1966. The United States delegate to the International Labor Organization (ILO) in Geneva, with Meany's support, boycotted its meetings because a Polish official had been elected as its presiding officer. The delegate argued that since Poland then had no free unions, the election made a mockery of the ILO's function as a discussion forum for trade union, government, and business representatives. Reuther fired off a letter deploring the "negative drift" of the AFL-CIO's views and criticizing the walkout as "unwise [and] undemocratic." If the United States government took a similar stand, he pointed out, the United Nations and nearly all other international organizations would cease to operate. The election of the Polish official had been open and democratic. As *The New York Times* commented, "Certainly no action by the American union delegation could have been more ironic: a walkout based on the vaunted abhorrence of United States labor for suppression of free decision-making and democratic choice in Eastern Europe." Recognizing that Reuther would receive little support within the AFL-CIO council and looking beyond the immediate issue to the growing opposition within the United States to the Vietnam War, the newspaper commended him for "the new respectability he has given the right to dissent."

The New York Times was correct in predicting that the council would line up behind Meany, although the 18–6 vote gave Reuther more support than he had expected. The meeting, as the paper said, was marked by "bitter exchanges" between the two adversaries. Meany, who wished to maintain a facade of unity, resented Reuther's decision to publicize differences through the press. Although the walkout won approval, Meany recognized that the fight would continue and that differences between the two were nearly irreconcilable. Asked by a reporter if he thought Reuther was qualified to succeed him, he roguishly replied, "I haven't any great interest in that because when that time comes, I won't be around." After the meeting, Meany agreed to Reuther's request for a thorough review of the AFL-CIO's foreign policy positions at a future session.

In August 1966 differences over Vietnam broke into the open. The AFL-CIO council adopted a statement that laid all the blame on the Communists for failure to begin negotiations, praised President Johnson for his willingness to use political pressure and military force, and denounced dissent at home. Furthermore, Meany announced that the statement had been unanimously approved. Reuther, who was not present because of a speaking engagement, attacked the statement as "intemperate, hysterical, jingoistic and unworthy of . . . a free labor movement." Explaining that if he had been present he would have opposed it, he pointed out that no one had been authorized to approve it for him.

When the council met for its review of foreign policy positions, Reuther did not attend. By then the UAW board had decided to take an independent position on political issues, and Reuther was determined to avoid association with unacceptable council statements. His absence was criticized by some—for example, Joe Curran, head of the Maritime Workers Union—

who had doubts about Meany's relentless bellicosity. Curran complained that Reuther "sold us down the river by not showing." With Reuther absent the council examined all its foreign policy positions since the merger and concluded smugly that it had a perfect record. After the meeting a reporter asked Meany if the council felt it had made "no mistakes whatsoever." "Yep," he answered, "we can't find any mistakes."

Reuther's withdrawal from council deliberations encouraged antiwar unionists to speak out. Within a few days an interunion coalition in New York City, including UAW members, attacked the war and the council's statement. Still Reuther refused to criticize President Johnson. Though urging him to end the bombing of North Vietnam in order to get negotiations underway and restating that "in the long pull, there are no military solutions to the problems of Asia," he declined to challenge the president directly.

In 1967 Senator Eugene McCarthy, followed by Senator Robert F. Kennedy after McCarthy's strong showing in the 1968 New Hampshire primary, rocked the Democratic party by attacking Johnson's war policy and announcing their candidacies for the presidential nomination. Johnson soon decided not to seek reelection. Since Reuther had long favored negotiations, and respected both McCarthy and Kennedy, he welcomed their new initiative. It is almost certain, as Victor Reuther avowed, that Walter eventually would have supported Kennedy, who had many admirers within the UAW's leadership and rank and file. Several officers, including Leonard Woodcock, Douglas Fraser, and Victor Reuther, endorsed Kennedy; but Walter for the moment made no move, out of respect for the long service to liberalism of Hubert Humphrey, now also a candidate. Kennedy's assassination in June 1968 foreclosed the need for a choice.

At the disorderly, strife-ridden Democratic convention, Reuther tried to obtain a compromise plank on Vietnam that would both draw back into the party those followers of McCarthy and Kennedy who were now drifting away and put an end to the fighting. Working both through the UAW and in cooperation with Clark Kerr, Norman Cousins, and others on the National Committee for a Political Settlement in Vietnam, he urged Humphrey, the platform committee, and the government's negotiators in Paris to commit themselves to an immediate standstill cease-fire; an international peacekeeping corps; free elections in South Vietnam with the protected participation of all, including Communists (whose victory he was prepared to risk, although he thought it unlikely); and extensive land redistribution. As part of the cease-fire, the bombing of North Vietnam would end with the "expectation" that North Vietnam would scale down its military activity. Humphrey was prepared to accept this program with one exception: bombing should continue until North Vietnam ended military action, still the Johnson administration's position.

With Richard Nixon the Republican candidate and Governor George Wallace of Alabama running on a third-party ticket, Reuther and the UAW endorsed Humphrey at a special conference of democratically elected delegates from UAW locals. Humphrey won the support of 88 percent of the delegates, Nixon 1 percent, and Wallace 10 percent. Although Reuther knew there would be no significant Nixon vote among auto workers, there was reason to fear that Wallace's campaign—aimed in part at exploiting the frustrations of white, northern blue-collar workers—would produce results. Bumper stickers bearing the message "U.A.W. Members Support Wallace for President" appeared in Detroit and other auto cities. Many journalists and pundits were predicting that Wallace's thinly disguised racist appeal, militaristic line on the war, and anti-government rhetoric would corral a large minority of auto workers' votes.

With some estimates placing Wallace's support as high as 25 percent of the electorate, which could have prevented either major candidate from gaining an electoral college majority and thrown the election into the House of Representatives, where Reuther feared that Wallace and Nixon supporters would cut a deal, the UAW launched its strongest-ever political campaign, targeting its efforts in states with concentrations of auto workers. Reuther attacked Wallace, charging that he was pushing the nation toward a "police state," and carefully recited the Alabama governor's antilabor and antiworker record. Auto workers were reminded that Wallace had raised "soak the poor" taxes, especially those on beer and tobacco; that Alabama's rates for workmen's and unemployment compensation were among the nation's lowest; that Wallace had refused to support repeal of the state's right-to-work law, which hampered union organizing; and that, despite strident appeals for "law and order" and sneers at tenderhearted liberals, Alabama had one of the country's highest crime rates. As election day approached, old habits reasserted themselves. Humphrey, whose chances had once been written off, cut deeply into Wallace's support in the northern states and nearly closed the gap on Nixon. The UAW's efforts made a significant contribution, with Humphrey carrying Michigan, for example, by two hundred thousand votes. Nationally, however, Nixon eked out a victory, a fitting climax to a decade of political frustration and disappointment for Reuther.

XI

Breaking Away

IN JULY 1968, five months before the presidential election, the UAW board decided to disaffiliate from the AFL-CIO. For nearly two years Reuther had openly discussed his "very fundamental trade union differences" with Meany, warning that the UAW was determined to take independent positions on foreign policy, civil rights, organizational drives, and other union and political issues. In a long statement prepared for UAW locals in December 1966, Reuther laid out his case against Meany's leadership. He lamented the federation's failure to fulfill its original promise, a "cause for grave concern." The AFL-CIO suffered from "a sense of complacency and adherence to the status quo"; it lacked "the social vision, the dynamic thrust, the crusading spirit that should characterize the progressive, modern labor movement." The statement prescribed new policy positions and structural reforms for the federation, including a recommendation that it develop stronger ties to the "liberal intellectual and academic community and among America's young people." The most severe strictures were reserved for the federation's "narrow and negative" anticommunism, which, Reuther charged, "has not strengthened but rather weakened the free world's efforts to resist Communism and all forms of tyranny." Repeating what had become a steady refrain, the letter continued: "The most effective way to fight Communism is to make democracy work. We believe that anticommunism in and of itself is not enough."

Soon after the issuance of this statement, ties between the UAW and the AFL-CIO began to snap. Reuther resigned from the council and its committees, with the exception of the presidency of the Industrial Union Department; and other UAW officers followed suit. Close observers of the situation believed that the UAW's secession was now inevitable. Yet Reuther moved slowly. Not until April 1967, when a UAW convention conferred authority on the board to withdraw from the federation, did Reuther publicly threaten to leave. He aimed to renew the labor movement, he said, but "this thing called labor unity is not a museum piece." If necessary, unity would be sacrificed to social commitment. "If we can get them all marching, so much the better. If we can't then we may have to make a decision to march alone, because," he told the cheering convention delegates, "we are determined to march one way or the other."

Meany, securely in control of the federation's council, was in no mood to confess failures or make concessions. Disdainful of Reuther and his concerns, he pointedly told reporters that discussion at a council meeting Reuther had not attended was "very very productive," and "on a very high level with practically nothing getting heated up or anything else." Dismissing Reuther's charges against his leadership as "baloney," Meany maintained that the trade union movement was "a more vital, a more vigorous and a more effective force for progress today than ever before in its history." The thrust of his defense was labor's prosperity: "Wages are higher, the fringe benefits are better, the contracts are better, the welfare and pension plans are better for the entire trade union movement."

Although Meany usually maintained his composure in these exchanges, his anger was aroused by challenges to his view of the Vietnam War. Emil Mazey helped to organize a meeting of the National Labor Leadership Assembly for Peace, attended by more than five hundred union officials including Victor Reuther, which denounced the war as immoral and called for a halt to American bombing. Shortly after, in a speech to an AFL-CIO convention, Meany sought to discredit the assembly's meeting with an unsubstantiated charge that it "was planned in Hanoi" and a false claim that its statement had been published two weeks before the meeting in the *Sunday Worker*, a Communist party paper. Mazey, a veteran of battles on both the platform and the picket line, accused Meany of deliberately lying and slandering fellow trade unionists.

Finally all hope of reconciliation was gone. When Reuther asked for a special AFL-CIO convention to consider his proposed reforms of the federation's structure and operations, Meany agreed, with the proviso that Reuther unconditionally promise in advance to accept its outcome. Reuther, of course, would not bind himself to accept an unsatisfactory result. The deadlock was broken in the spring of 1968, when the UAW ceased to pay the per capita tax on its membership owed to the AFL-CIO. Reuther may have hoped that the UAW would be allowed to remain in limbo—neither in nor out of the federation—until after the presidential election; but the council at Meany's direction voted for suspension, and the UAW board thereupon disaffiliated.

When the UAW pulled out of the AFL-CIO, it went alone. Reuther's failure to enlist any of the CIO unions in his crusade for labor's revitalization was a serious setback. The UAW's isolation made it easy to dismiss his protest against Meany's leadership as a personal quarrel, and the credibility of his charges was diminished when other unions, including some that once were close to the UAW, failed to respond. Some labor leaders took exception to Reuther's public attacks, believing that criticisms should have been aired only in private. Others were annoyed with what they saw as a lack of follow-through after charges were made. Doubtless many were simply comfortable with Meany's direction of the federation.

Meany shrewdly exploited opportunities to defend his position. For example, he cultivated the support of I. W. Abel, the new president of the United Steel Workers, whose social and political outlook was close to Reuther's, tacitly allowing that if a break with Reuther occurred, Abel would become the number-two man in the AFL-CIO. After the UAW disaffiliated, Abel succeeded Reuther as president of the Industrial Union Department. As a union politician, George Meany may have been more than a match for Reuther.

More significant than Meany's countermeasures, however, was Reuther's laxity in building support. In a lapse from his usual realistic analysis of a situation and attention to detail, he naively believed that his critique of Meany's leadership was so palpably true that liberal labor leaders would have to rally to the cause. The isolation into which he maneuvered himself was costly to the measures he supported.

Only weeks after leaving the AFL-CIO Reuther tried to break out of this isolation and create a new platform for expounding labor's position on political issues by launching a new organization, the Alliance for Labor Action. The ALA was not a rival federation, although Meany branded it a dual union and threatened to expel AFL-CIO affiliates that joined. The alliance was limited to coordination of organizing campaigns and of political positions and activities. The unlikely partner in this venture was the International Brotherhood of Teamsters, whose president, Jimmy Hoffa, was then in prison. Although it seemed odd for Reuther to join with the union whose expulsion from the AFL-CIO he had helped bring about, and there were astonished gasps when the alliance's formation was announced, their cooperation was neither farfetched nor, while it lasted, ineffective. Reuther had long known fellow Detroiters Hoffa and Frank Fitzsimmons, the teamsters' acting president. Locally the two unions had erratic—sometimes friendly and sometimes hostile—relations. Both had a strong commitment to organizing unorganized workers, and in a key concession the teamsters' leadership agreed to follow Reuther's lead on the political and social questions that were so important to him. Although membership in the alliance was open to any union, and two other small organizations joined, even by themselves the auto workers and the teamsters formed a powerful combination. With nearly 2 million members, the teamsters were the largest union in the nation, and the 1.5-million-member UAW was not far behind.

With the persistence of the war, the formation of the ALA, and Richard Nixon in the White House, Reuther stepped up his criticisms of the United States' Vietnam policy. In the fall of 1969, with UAW board approval, he supported the peaceful antiwar demonstrations of the Vietnam Moratorium with newspaper ads and funds, and, for the first time, endorsed complete and early American withdrawal from the war. An ALA statement called on "our Government to face up to the reality that there is nothing to be won in Vietnam that is worth one more drop of American blood." The organization, it added, took its stand "with those who are for getting out quickly and completely."

At the UAW convention in the spring of 1970—the last he was to attend—Reuther condemned the war for dividing the nation, wasting its resources, and tarnishing its moral credentials. He did not condone illegal acts of protest or anti-American radicalism, however. "I want to make it clear," he said, that "we condemn those Americans who burn the American flag and march behind the Viet Cong flag. We reject the concept that says in order to be antiwar you have to be anti-American." A few days later, when Nixon's invasion of Cambodia provoked massive demonstrations resulting in the deaths of four students at Kent State University, Reuther undertook to organize a national coalition against violence, an effort cut short by his death.

The UAW and the ALA were also early opponents of the Nixon administration's plan for an immensely expensive anti-ballistic missile system, and Reuther endorsed proposals urging Nixon to begin negotiations to prevent the spread of nuclear weapons and for arms limitations. The UAW's withdrawal from the AFL-CIO broke the united front of labor's support for the war and huge military expenditures and began the renewal of labor's fragmented ties with other elements of the liberal community.

With the war gradually winding down, Reuther became concerned about the economic consequences of peace. Since many

Vietnam military contractors had little experience with production for civilian markets, he feared that their reluctance to test
those hazardous waters might perpetuate the military-industrial
complex. He was ready with a plan. In testimony before the
Senate Labor and Public Welfare Committee, he proposed that
military contractors be required to put one-quarter of their after-
tax profits from war production into a government trust fund.
The money would be used to finance retraining and family
benefits for workers displaced by cancellation of military contracts. As an incentive to encourage companies to plan for the
transition to peacetime production, any amounts remaining in
the fund would be returned to them as profits. When Senator
Thomas Eagleton of Missouri asked Reuther whether persuasion rather than the threat of withheld profits would not be
adequate to secure cooperation, Reuther replied that thirty years
at the bargaining table had convinced him that "only the threat
to their profits moves them." Although seven Democratic senators on the committee endorsed the plan in varying degrees, and
The New York Times commended Reuther for trying to goad
government, business, and labor into constructive thinking on
the postwar economy, nothing more was heard of it in Congress
or the Nixon administration.

The union's relationship with the auto manufacturers was
complicated by the emergence of new concerns over car design
and the impact of a changing car market. With the publication of
Ralph Nader's study, *Unsafe at Any Speed* in 1965, the question of
car safety became a significant national issue for the first time.
Soon major safety legislation was under consideration. Reuther
submitted a statement to Congress backing mandatory safety
standards and the establishment of a national system of car
inspection. The manufacturers, he remarked, seemed more
interested in "jazzing up" cars than in safety devices. Profits, he
added, could meet the cost of safety equipment and inspection.
"It is difficult for concerned and responsible persons," he wrote,
"to understand the reluctance of the auto industry to accept the
conclusions of numerous safety experts and apply them to

design." Although Reuther readily castigated the manufacturers for their sins, a sensitive aspect of the problem was the popular suspicion that careless assembly line workers were partly to blame for car accidents and fatalities. Uncharacteristically, Reuther declined to testify on car safety in person before Congress, prompting press speculation that he wished to avoid questions about the possible role of auto workers in producing unsafe cars.

Reuther aroused the ire of company presidents and industry spokesmen by assuming that profits were sufficient to meet added expenses, but he was concerned over the long-range financial threat to the companies and the work force from increasing foreign competition. Although employment and profits in the domestic industry remained high beyond the end of the decade, Reuther recognized that foreign manufacturers had made serious and perhaps permanent inroads into the United States market. Therefore, he pursued remedies on several fronts.

As early as 1962 Reuther persuaded the UAW convention to authorize a contribution of $1.5 million to a Free World Labor Fund that would be used to "support international solidarity among workers, to equip the International Metalworkers Federation to carry out organizing tasks and to promote higher wages and improved working conditions for workers in foreign countries." Later that year he visited Japan—one of the first American working-class representatives to do so—at the invitation of its union leaders. There he urged them to follow the example of American unions in severing ties with communist organizations in order to concentrate on improving wages and working conditions.

As he had before, Reuther urged the manufacturers to meet foreign competition head on by offering a comparable product. In 1965, partly with a view to finding employment for the several thousand UAW members who had lost jobs when Studebaker pulled out of the automobile business, Reuther made the unorthodox proposal of allowing the remaining United States manufacturers to establish jointly a new corporation that would produce a small car, competitive in price and quality with the Volkswagen and similar imports. The costs of design, development, and manufacture would be substantially reduced and a car quickly brought to market. President Johnson, on whom Reuther repeatedly pressed the idea, was drawn to it; but the Justice Department's argument that it would require repeal of the antitrust laws, something no one but Reuther was prepared to take up wth Congress, ended consideration.

By the end of the decade the problem was worsening. Reuther recognized that the auto workers themselves would have to exercise restraint as a contribution to equalizing costs, and he did not refrain from pointing out this unpleasant truth to his constituency. Although the most substantial effects of foreign competition on auto employment were still in the future, Reuther warned a UAW skilled-trades conference in 1970 that American auto workers no longer possessed a monopoly of the domestic automobile labor market. Their bargaining power was correspondingly reduced, setting closer limits to their likely gains in future negotiations. Comparing auto work with the building trades, he said: "They have a monopoly. You can't build a skyscraper that you need in New York in Japan, but you can build automobiles in Japan and you can make tools and dies in Japan." As the oil shortages, inflation, and high interest rates of coming years painfully demonstrated, both the auto companies and auto workers were vulnerable to the lower costs of foreign manufacturers.

Restraint could not easily be taught to a membership whose experience had led it to expect a constantly rising standard of living. During the 1960s the UAW continued to press for higher wages and other monetary returns, but improvements in working conditions received more emphasis. In 1964, for example, differences with GM over production standards—mainly the pace and amount of work to be performed—provoked a national strike. Within a month more than half of the GM workers had ratified the contract, thus ending the national strike; but workers in twenty-eight GM plants stayed out for varying periods of time because of unsettled production standards and local grievance issues. In addition to a wage settlement calling for a 60-cent-an-hour increase spread over three years and a cost-of-living adjustment of another 10 cents an hour, the 1964 contracts also contained early retirement incentives, improved pensions, longer vacations, improved insurance benefits, and additional daily relief time for some workers.

Ford was selected as the target in 1967. The union proposed a wage and benefit package that amounted to 90 cents an hour, and the company responded with an offer of about two-thirds that amount. In prestrike negotiations neither side made any important concessions. The strike against Ford began on September 6, just as the new 1968 models were being launched, and lasted until October 12. With a strike fund of $67 million, the union was well prepared. Although Ford officials had denounced the UAW's demands as unconscionable, the settlement was a substantial victory for the union. The guaranteed annual wage, which the UAW had pursued for more than a dozen years, was achieved. Workers with seven years seniority were now guaranteed 95 percent of their pay, including unemployment benefits, for up to a year, less a small amount to compensate for savings in lunch and travel costs. The wage settlement met most of the demands of the skilled workers, who had seen the differential between their pay and that of production workers shrink over the years. They received an increase of 50 cents an hour, whereas production workers gained a 20-cent-an-hour raise. Nevertheless, in separate ratification votes the skilled workers approved the contract by a three-to-one margin, with production workers voting for it by an overwhelming nine to one.

Reuther made an important concession to Ford in order to obtain this favorable settlement: he agreed to an annual 8-cent-an-hour ceiling on cost-of-living increases over the life of the contract. With the nation's overheated economy on the verge of an inflationary spiral due primarily to unchecked rising military and other government spending, this concession proved costly.

Reuther later admitted he had erred in agreeing to it, although holding out could have prolonged the strike for weeks. Measured by the previous COLA formula, the ceiling cost each worker between $700 and $1,000 over the three years of the contract, resulted in a loss in real wages for that period, and saved the companies hundreds of millions of dollars.

While attending to bargaining responsibilities, Reuther never failed to remind the UAW's members of the limits of bread-and-butter unionism. He knew that the larger environment, beyond the direct reach of negotiations, could have a profound impact on the workers' lives. At the 1968 convention he asked: "What good is a large wage increase if the world goes up, or a guaranteed annual wage if the neighborhood or city burns, or a large pension if the streets are unsafe, or a long vacation if the air is poisoned and water polluted?"

Race and class conflict, so destructively expressed in the riots that convulsed Harlem, Watts, Newark, Detroit, and other cities between 1965 and the end of the decade, was the most devastating domestic problem. Reuther and the UAW had strongly supported civil rights and antipoverty programs to get at its roots, but unions might make a more direct contribution. The ghetto eruptions, Reuther thought, stemmed in large part from social fragmentation and the frustration of powerlessness—a situation not unlike that of industrial workers before the formation of unions. Working with Jack Conway—a former assistant and long-time associate in social and political causes—and through the Industrial Union Department and the UAW, Reuther helped to launch several experiments in the development of community unions, an adaptation of the trade union for purposes of community betterment. In 1967 Reuther wrote: "A new concept of union organization has been developing. . . . Properly nurtured and motivated, it can spread across the face of the nation, changing the social character of the inner city structure and uplifting the lives of millions of slum dwellers." Conway added: "We believe that just as the auto worker and the steel worker . . . gained self-respect and dignity through organization, so, too, can the poor gain self-respect and dignity by the same methods." Community unions would be part union and part community organizations, bringing residents together to bargain with landlords, the police, and other providers of services. They would start and administer educational and retraining programs and would engage in political activity.

Characterized as "one of the most imaginative ideas to emerge from organized labor in the postwar period," community unions were established in ghettos in Chicago, Newark, and Watts. They faced serious challenges. Reliable and skillful leadership was difficult to find and develop, except in Watts, where a UAW steward, Ted Watkins, was energetic and resourceful. The community unions became entangled in rivalries with civil rights, ethnic, and political organizations competing for community support and funds. If they succeeded in attracting government or foundation money, their functions as manager and disburser of funds tended to overshadow community organization and other kinds of service. Although none of the experimental groups fulfilled the hopes of Reuther and Conway by becoming permanent organizations of community residents, they did succeed for a time in drawing together a portion of the urban underclass in pursuit of common goals of betterment.

Within the UAW, as in most of the large industrial unions that had been established in the 1930s, the potential for class, racial, and generational conflict increased in the 1960s, becoming so serious that the solidarity of the work force and the credibility of the union with some of its members were called into question. The heightening of tensions coincided with—and in part reflected—a transformation of the union's composition. Between 1962 and 1967 the UAW admitted 842,000 new members, over half its entire number; by 1970 one-third of the members had less than five years' seniority. Among both the rank and file and the leadership cadres in the locals, the generation that had been present when lasting loyalties were formed at the creation of the union was rapidly passing out of the plants. Only in the upper levels of the international union were there still many familiar faces, a fact that might only intensify the alienation from authority felt in the ranks.

The commitment of the UAW and Reuther to racial equality on the job and civil rights did not insulate the union from the challenges of dissatisfied black workers. A long history of injustice in the auto plants, stretching back to the wartime strikes, the riot of 1943, and even earlier, fed black discontent. In the plants black workers had often been exposed to unfair and offensive instances of racism. Since World War II the UAW had attacked racism within its ranks through policies and educational programs with more determination, perhaps, than any other major union. Although it is impossible to measure the change in behavior these programs brought about, and obviously they did not eliminate the problem, injustice and racial tension within the union and the plants would surely have been much worse without them.

Employment of blacks in the auto industry and the percentage of black members in the UAW increased. By 1968 blacks made up 19 percent of the blue-collar work force of the Big Three (they constituted a mere 2.4 percent of the white-collar, almost entirely nonunion, occupational groups in the industry, with the majority of these holding clerical positions). In blue-collar occupations the distribution of blacks varied from a low of 3 percent among skilled craftsmen, to 21 percent of operatives (the largest category with more than half a million employees), to 27 percent and 29 percent for the smaller numbers of service workers and laborers, respectively. Although the UAW kept no records of its members' race, UAW sources estimated that approximately 18 percent were blacks by the end of the decade. Estimates by others ranged as high as 25 percent.

For years black unionists had pointed out that, given their numbers in the union, they had little representation in the leadership. Locals with substantial numbers of black members, such as Local 600, had some black officers; and blacks would be found among their delegates to conventions. By the end of the

1960s eleven locals in the Detroit area, where black members were concentrated, had black presidents, and there were hundreds of black lesser officials such as shop committee members and stewards. However, as late as 1968 only 7 percent of the representatives and other staff officers in the international were black.

The Trade Union Leadership Council (TULC) was formed in Detroit in 1958 to bring blacks into leadership positions in unions and politics. Although its activities extended beyond the UAW, most of its membership came from the union. Its two leading figures, Horace Sheffield and Robert "Buddy" Battle 3d, were well-known black UAW unionists. Sheffield was on the UAW staff and had been a supporter of Reuther's since the struggle with the Thomas-Addes faction, and Battle was the head of the largely black division of foundry workers at Ford's. TULC was integrationist. It invited white unionists to join, and a number of white UAW officials and staff members, including friends of Reuther's, responded. Its membership, however, which once numbered 7,000, was predominantly black.

One of TULC's immediate objectives was to secure an executive board position for a black. At the 1959 convention Sheffield, without obtaining Reuther's approval, nominated Willoughby Abner, a black UAW unionist from Chicago, for the board. Despite the urgings of some members of his caucus, Reuther refused to fire Sheffield from the UAW staff for insubordination. In 1962 Nelson Jack Edwards, a TULC member, was elected to the board as a member at large by the entire convention. In 1968 Marcellius Ivory of Local 600 was chosen as a regional director by his region's delegates. Although it cannot be said that the UAW practiced equality in its treatment of black members, it did more than any other major union to open the way for blacks to positions of responsibility and leadership. Its actions in this respect compared favorably with those of business, educational, political, and government institutions.

When riots and radical black nationalism swept American ghettos in the late 1960s, the UAW's constructive record on race, the generally high average incomes of black auto workers, and the presence of a large black middle class in Detroit tempted many to believe the city would be spared. In July 1967, however, the worst riot in the twentieth-century United States shattered that illusion. During the Detroit riot there was no disorder in the factories, but the effects of racial tension and black militancy were soon evident.

In the riot's aftermath, the auto companies, and the union—which had long recognized the validity of the charge of unequal employment opportunity and had tried to do something about it—joined in a response. Since the employers controlled hiring, the main responsibility fell on them. Various methods were tried to increase black employment—particularly among ghetto youth and the hard-core unemployed—and to recruit candidates for apprenticeships in the skilled trades. By the end of 1967 GM had hired 5,000 blacks in the Detroit area out of a total of 12,000 newly hired workers. By 1969 Ford had hired 13,000 of the formerly hard-core unemployed. Chrysler, cooperating with the UAW, established a training program for skilled-trades workers that brought in over 4,000 blacks in two years. According to one study, "the most substantial improvements . . . in the country for black blue-collar workers" were made in the Detroit-area Chrysler plants at the end of the decade.

As always, social intent was conditioned by resistant economic and political realities. The Chrysler program, which relied partly on federal funds, lost the bulk of them during the Nixon administration. When demand for cars declined in 1969, Ford and Chrysler began to lay off many recently hired workers under contract seniority rules. For black workers the adage, "last hired, first fired," still applied. Appalled at the social and economic injustice and waste involved, the UAW proposed a "juniority" or "inverse seniority" plan whereby older workers with high seniority, eligible for SUB and unemployment compensation benefits, could volunteer for layoff, thus protecting the jobs of younger, recently hired black and white workers. The plan, however, was rejected by the auto companies, which claimed that the increase in labor costs resulting from the replacement of trained, disciplined, and reliable older workers with younger ones made it uneconomical. Already disadvantaged on costs in competition with foreign-made cars, they were reluctant to add to their problems. The black employment picture had improved, but less than was hoped or had seemed possible.

The riot also brought to the surface revolutionary organizations among militant blacks. In 1968 DRUM (Dodge Revolutionary Union Movement), the first of several Marxist-oriented black workers' organizations, emerged in the vast Dodge Main plant in Hamtramck, where more than half of the 7,000 employees were blacks. It was followed by ELRUM (Eldon Revolutionary Union Movement) at a Chrysler gear and axle plant and about a dozen others elsewhere, all eventually allied in the League of Revolutionary Black Workers. They published leaflets and papers attacking the racist practices of employers and the unions; denounced the "Uncle Toms" who were loyal to the UAW; brought up job grievances over unsafe and harmful working conditions that the companies and, they charged, the union had ignored; held rallies; and called wildcat strikes. They directed their fire equally at the companies and the UAW, which they claimed conspired against the interests of ordinary workers. DRUM denounced Reuther and local UAW officials as racists, and the league urged that Reuther be fired and that half of the UAW's board and staff positions be designated for blacks. "Behead the Redhead," said one leaflet. DRUM also demanded that Chrysler promote fifty blacks to foremen's positions at Dodge Main and name blacks as plant manager and chairman of the corporation's board of directors.

Rhetorical overkill, ideological extremism, and flirtation with violence (a DRUM fundraising raffle offered an M-1 rifle as first prize), circumscribed these organizations' appeal. Attempts to move into union electoral politics by running candidates and slates in local elections produced negligible results. UAW leaders denounced them for attempting to divide the work force on racial lines, arguing that only the union's traditional integrationist position would solve their problems as workers and as blacks. As Reuther said in 1970 in his last major speech at a UAW convention: "There are no white answers to the problems. There are no black answers. There are only common answers that we must plan together in the solidarity of our common humanity."

Although some progress had been made, dominance of local union offices by one race with tokenism for the other was often the pattern. That is, divided locals in which blacks were the majority would elect black officers and a token white, with the reverse happening in locals with a white majority. Racial tension and prejudice remained high in some plants and locals, and verbal clashes and physical assaults occurred. After the assassination of Martin Luther King in 1968, workers at two plants threatened wildcat strikes if flags were lowered to half mast as many blacks were demanding.

Still, the extent of racial division should not be overdrawn. Whites and blacks normally worked side by side without friction and cooperated in union matters with little regard to race. By Reuther's death in 1970 the UAW, the economic and political instrument of the auto work force, was the largest and most powerful, genuinely if imperfectly, racially integrated private organization in the United States. Even on social—as distinguished from economic—questions, UAW blue-collar workers were often in advance of the general population. In 1968 *The New York Times* reported, Flint, Michigan, populated largely by GM workers and their families, adopted "the first open housing measure ever approved by a popular referendum."

As memories of the depression and the union's early days dimmed, age, race, gender, skill, and other divisions within the work force became more evident and significant. The relaxation of the bonds of common struggle threatened to undermine solidarity, a problem for other unions as well as the UAW. The problem was not entirely the result of institutional inertia or an unresponsive leadership. In part, it could be traced to the unions' success. As union members gained the income security, status, and standard of living of the middle class, their bonds with all expressions and instruments of working-class culture, including unions, weakened. Furthermore, gains in income allowed workers to shift their attention and demands for improvements to working conditions, in some ways a more difficult matter for unions to deal with. Part of the problem also resulted from modern society's heavily promoted devotion to the value of upward mobility, which made class organizations something to escape from rather than find fulfillment in. In any case, workers' morale and commitment to unions declined.

Reuther had long been aware of the need to "unionize the organized" as the work force renewed itself. Characteristically, his approach was not a negative or self-pitying condemnation of those who took for granted the sacrifices and achievements of their predecessors. Rather, he sought to attack the problem positively through a new concept of worker's education designed to meet the needs of new generations. A deliberate, rational effort could be made to renew commitment at all levels and nurture future leaders.

Realistically, Reuther knew that the development of leaders and members to their full union potential required the allegiance of both the worker and the worker's family. Reuther's experience provided ample confirmation: May Reuther, his wife, had been as devoted to the union cause as her husband; the marriages of Victor and Roy similarly rested on a foundation of shared commitment to union values and liberal activism. If the union was to represent a way of life, it had to be anchored in the family as well as in the workplace.

With these thoughts in mind, Reuther committed the UAW, despite doubts and reservations among portions of both its leadership and the ranks, to the purchase of a large, scenic tract of land on Black Lake in northern Michigan for the construction of a Family Education Center. The building of the center, in which he took a close interest, was the last project of his life. The recreational and living facilities were superb, but it was not meant to be a summer resort for vacationing workers. Those who had demonstrated an interest in the union's effectiveness and future were eligible to apply. Under the UAW's Education Department the center conducted a wide range of activities to train future union activists; examine the political, social, and economic questions facing the union; and give the participants an opportunity to respond with their ideas and concerns. The center was dedicated to the proposition that open communication and constructive, cooperative thought would continually reknit the ties between worker and union.

Reuther did not live to see the Family Education Center completed. On the night of May 9, 1970, Walter and May—accompanied by Billy Wolfman, Reuther's bodyguard and nephew, and Oscar Stonorov, the center's architect—left Detroit for Black Lake in a chartered jet with two experienced pilots for a weekend's inspection. As the plane approached the airport at Pellston, Michigan, beneath an 800 foot ceiling and a light rain, it clipped the top of a tree and crashed in flames. All those aboard were killed immediately. A government investigation pointed to a faulty altimeter as the accident's most likely cause. When the memorial service began a few days later in Detroit, the nation's auto factories fell silent as assembly lines, presses, and lathes halted. For three minutes men and machines stood motionless.

Reuther's unexpected death sent a shock through the UAW. With contracts due to expire and negotiations imminent, however, the union quickly and smoothly selected a new president. Two able, experienced lieutenants, Leonard Woodcock and Douglas Fraser, were the candidates. The board was almost evenly divided between them; yet the choice of Woodcock, the older man, was made without rancor. Since Reuther had emphasized teamwork in the leadership, that outcome was not surprising.

As a UAW founder and an officer for thirty-five years, including twenty-four as its president, Reuther secured those material means to a better life that the union's members wanted. In many respects the UAW set the pace for a generation of workers in winning compensation that raised living standards, enhanced economic security, provided opportunities for workers' families, and added to self-respect. The auto workers' cities lacked glamour but were generally prosperous. During Reuther's presidency, both Detroit and Flint consistently ranked high among American cities and metropolitan areas of their size in average family income.

Reuther had always maintained that a responsible vital union would contribute ideas and perspectives to the industry's and the nation's welfare. When, after his death, the industry confronted problems caused by higher fuel costs, obsolete products and plants, shifting and unstable demand, and uncompetitively high manufacturing (including labor) costs, the need to recognize common interests among workers, management, and the public became all the more important. Hard times weakened management's resistance to sharing authority. In 1979–1980 Chrysler Corporation, facing bankruptcy, added the UAW's president to its board of directors and renegotiated its labor contract to reduce costs. A Ford executive, whose company soon successfully sought a new, reduced-cost contract, told a reporter: "Let's face it. Our system of 'laissez-faire' private enterprise has run its course. Government, industry and unions have to work together now. It's what people like me used to condemn as socialism." "Both labor and management," Reuther once wrote, "while they have separate responsibilities also have a joint responsibility to the whole of society; the joint responsibility to the whole transcends their separate responsibilities." No one can say what contributions Reuther would have made to solving the difficult problems facing the modern auto industry. What can be said with certainty is that he would have had a plan.

Reuther was the leading American advocate and practitioner of social unionism—the use of unions to pursue the public good through political, social, and economic reforms. As The New York Times wrote shortly after his death, he was "the most zealous union proponent of the concept that labor must go forward with the community and not at the expense of the community." His place as a labor leader, it continued, would be hard to fill; but "the void will be greater still in the realms of idealism and social inventiveness." Reuther's idealism and inventiveness were products of the American working-class experience, a creative adaptation of social-democratic perspectives to American conditions and realities, manifested not only in words, but also in the daily lives of millions.

A Note on the Sources

ABUNDANT PRIMARY SOURCES exist for the study of Reuther and the history of the UAW. By far the most valuable and extensive collections are in the Archives of Labor History and Urban Affairs, Wayne State University, which since 1962 has been the official depository for UAW records. The records of the international union's departments and offices, of dozens of UAW locals, and the papers of numerous UAW figures are available there. The most important collection for this study was the Walter P. Reuther Papers, consisting of office records and memoranda, reports, and correspondence. Other valuable collections included the papers of George Addes, Merlin D. Bishop, Joe Brown, Richard T. Frankensteen, Nat Ganley, Henry Kraus, Homer Martin, Victor Reuther, Maurice Sugar, and R. J. Thomas. The UAW–General Motors Department collection is good for information on the period when Reuther was its director. Other materials at the archives include the Reuther Biography File, and the CIO Secretary-Treasurer (James B. Carey) Collection, which includes the minutes of the CIO executive board. Copies of the minutes of the UAW general executive board may be found in several collections. The archives has a collection of transcribed interviews. Among those used were interviews with George Addes, John W. Anderson, Merlin D. Bishop, Arthur Case, James M. Cleveland, Dick Coleman, Bert Foster, Everett Francis, Richard T. Frankensteen, Nat Ganley, William Genske, Carl Haessler, Matthew B. Hammond, Tom Klasey, Theodore LaDuke, John McGill, George Merrelli, Ken Morris, F. R. "Jack" Palmer, William Stevenson, Shelton Tappes, R. J. Thomas, Ray Vess, and Leonard Woodcock. For descriptions of the archives collections as of 1974, see Warner F. Pflug, compiler and editor, *A Guide to the Archives of Labor History and Urban Affairs, Wayne State University* (Detroit: Wayne State University Press, 1974).

Useful manuscript collections elsewhere were the Congress of Industrial Organizations Collection, Catholic University of America, the Eleanor Roosevelt Papers and the Henry Morganthau, Jr., Diary at the Franklin D. Roosevelt Library, the Socialist Party of America Collection at Duke University, the Norman Thomas papers at the New York Public Library, and the War Production Board Records in the National Archives. The papers of GM president Charles E. Wilson at Anderson College, Anderson, Indiana, yielded little on this subject.

Indispensable printed sources include the *Proceedings* of the UAW's conventions between 1936 and 1970 and the reports of its presidents to the conventions (variously titled). The record of CIO and, after 1955, AFL-CIO convention *Proceedings* is also important.

Newspapers and other periodicals were invaluable. *The New York Times*, the *Detroit News*, and the *Detroit Free Press* provided the most detailed and consecutive coverage. Others that were useful included the *Detroit Times, New York Herald Tribune, New York Post, PM,* and the *Washington Post.* Detailed accounts of UAW conventions were sometimes available in newspapers of the host cities, such as the *Atlantic City Evening Bulletin* and the *Buffalo Courier-Express.* Among union newspapers were the *United Automobile Worker,* the *West Side Conveyor* (from Reuther's home Local 174), *Ammunition,* and the *CIO News.* Another valuable labor paper that circulated in the Detroit area was the *Wage Earner,* published by the Association of Catholic Trade Unionists, and its predecessor, the *Michigan Labor Leader.* Both were usually friendly to Reuther. Not so friendly were accounts and editorials appearing in the *Daily Worker* and the *Daily People's World.* Periodicals that carried articles on the auto industry and the UAW included *Business Week, Fortune,* the *Nation,* the *New Leader,* the *New Republic,* the *Socialist Appeal,* and the *Socialist Call.* A file of the *Moscow Daily News,* 1934–1935, which printed letters from Reuther when he was working at the Gorki plant, is available at the Library of Congress.

A convenient collection of twenty-one statements by Reuther—on topics ranging from the 500-planes-a-day plan in 1940 to a Mike Wallace interview in 1960—is Henry P. Christman, editor, *Walter P. Reuther; Selected Papers* (New York: Macmillan Company, 1961). Among the few publications bearing Reuther's name as author are *500 Planes a Day: A Program for the Utilization of the Automobile Industry for Mass Production of Defense Planes* (Washington, D.C.: American Council on Public Affairs, [1940]); *Purchasing Power for Prosperity; The Case of the General Motors Workers for Maintaining Take-Home Pay* (Detroit: International Union, UAW-CIO, General Motors Department, 1945); and "How to Beat the Communists," *Collier's*, February 28, 1948.

Among biographical and autobiographical accounts, the most important is Victor G. Reuther, *The Brothers Reuther and the Story of the UAW/A Memoir* (Boston: Houghton Mifflin, 1976). Many of the subjects dealt with in this book that involved close association between the brothers are discussed there in detail. A thoughtful and still valuable work on the first decade of the UAW's history is Irving Howe and B. J. Widick, *The UAW and Walter Reuther* (New York: Random House, 1949; reprinted New York: DaCapo Press, 1973). The two book-length biographies are Frank Cormier and William J. Eaton, *Reuther* (Englewood Cliffs, N.J.: Prentice-Hall, 1970), and Jean Gould and Lorena Hickok, *Walter Reuther: Labor's Rugged Individualist* (New York: Dodd, Mead, 1972), both rushed into print shortly after Reuther's death. Transcripts of the interviews conducted by Cormier and Eaton with Reuther and many associates are in the John F. Kennedy Presidential Library, Boston. Two brief studies—Fred J. Cook, *Building the House of Labor: Walter Reuther* (Chicago, New York, London: Encyclopaedia Britannica Press, 1963), and Robert L. Tyler, *Walter Reuther* (Grand Rapids, Mich.: W. B. Eerdmans, 1973)—add little. A leading instance of a hostile study is Eldorus L. Dayton, *Walter Reuther: Autocrat of the Bargaining Table* (New York: Devin-Adair, 1958).

Several biographical essays and studies of particular subjects are useful. See especially Murray Kempton, "Father and Sons (the Reuther Boys)," in *Part of Our Time: Some Ruins and Monuments of the Thirties* (New York: Simon and Schuster, 1955), pp. 261–298; C. Wright Mills, *The New Men of Power: America's Labor Leaders* (New York: Harcourt, Brace, 1948); Daniel Bell, "Labor's New Men of Power," *Fortune*, June 1953; B. J. Widick, "Walter P. Reuther," in *Labor Today; The Triumphs and Failures of Unionism in the United States* (Boston: Houghton Mifflin, 1964), pp. 181–229; George R. Clark, "The Strange Story of the Reuther Plan," *Harper's Magazine*, May 1942, pp. 645–654; and Alfred O. Hero, *The Reuther-Meany Foreign Policy Dispute* (Dobbs Ferry, N.Y.: Oceana Publications, 1970). The Reuther Biography File at the Archives of Labor History and Urban Affairs contains copies of several biographical articles and essays, mostly from popular periodicals of the postwar period.

Although there is no general scholarly study of the UAW's history, some portions of the story, especially during the 1930s, have received careful scrutiny. Outstanding are the works of Sidney Fine. See particularly *Sit-Down: The General Motors Strike of 1936–1937* (Ann Arbor: University of Michigan Press, 1969); *The Automobile Under the Blue Eagle* (Ann Arbor: University of Michigan Press, 1963); *Frank Murphy: The Detroit Years* (Ann Arbor: University of Michigan Press, 1975); *Frank Murphy: The New Deal Years* (Chicago: University of Chicago Press, 1979); "The Origins of the United Automobile Workers, 1933–1935," *Journal of Economic History* 18, no. 3 (September 1958): 249–282; "The Toledo Chevrolet Strike of 1935," *Ohio Historical Quarterly* 67, no. 4 (October 1958): 326–356; and "The Tool and Die Makers Strike of 1933," *Michigan History* 42, no. 3 (September 1958): 297–323.

An illuminating approach to the union's history is taken in Warner F. Pflug, *The UAW in Pictures* (Detroit: Wayne State University Press, 1971). Memoirs by UAW activists include Clayton W. Fountain, *Union Guy* (New York: Viking Press, 1949), by a Reuther associate; Frank Marquart, *An Auto Worker's Journal: The UAW from Crusade to One-Party Union* (University Park: Pennsylvania State University Press, 1975), by a socialist critic; John W. Anderson, "How I Became Part of the Labor Movement," in Alice Lynd and Staughton Lynd, eds., *Rank and File: Personal Histories by Working Class Organizers* (Boston: Beacon Press, 1973), pp. 37–66; and Wyndham Mortimer, *Organize! My Life as a Union Man* (Boston: Beacon Press, 1971), an account by the one-time UAW vice-president. An interesting comparison of auto workers in Flint, Michigan, and Coventry, England—emphasizing the impact of different kinds of class consciousness on organization—is in Ronald Edsforth, "Divergent Traditions in Union Organization in the Automobile Industries of Flint, Michigan and Coventry, England," *Detroit in Perspective: A Journal of Regional History* 5, no. 3 (Spring 1981): 2–20. Other studies are George D. Blackwood, "The United Automobile Workers of America, 1935–1951," Ph.D. dissertation, University of Chicago, 1952; Peter Friedlander, *The Emergence of a UAW Local, 1936–1939: A Study in Class and Culture* (Pittsburgh: University of Pittsburgh Press, 1975); William Serrin, *The Company and the Union* (New York: Knopf, 1973), a study of the General Motors strike of 1970; the always useful Jack Stieber, *Governing the UAW* (New York and London: Wiley, 1962); and B. J. Widick, *Detroit: City of Race and Class Violence* (Chicago: Quadrangle, 1972).

The factional struggles of the union's early years may be followed in Walter Galenson, "The Automobile Industry," in *The CIO Challenge to the*

AFL (Cambridge, Mass.: Harvard University Press, 1960), pp. 123–192, a detailed and fair account; Ray Boryczka, "Seasons of Discontent: Auto Union Factionalism and the Motor Products Strike of 1936–37," *Michigan History* 61, no. 1 (Spring 1977): 3–32; and "Militancy and Factionalism in the United Auto Workers Union, 1937–1941," *The Maryland Historian* 8, no. 2 (Fall 1977): 13–25; Lorin L. Cary, "Institutionalized Conservatism in the Early C.I.O.: Adolph Germer, a Case Study," *Labor History* 13, no. 4 (Fall 1972): 475–504; Henry Kraus, *The Many and the Few: A Chronicle of the Dynamic Auto Workers* (Los Angeles: Plantin Press, 1947), a participant's history of the Flint sitdown; Jack W. Skeels, "The Development of Political Stability Within the United Automobile Workers Union," Ph.D. dissertation, University of Wisconsin, 1957; and Jack W. Skeels, "The Background of UAW Factionalism," *Labor History* 2, no. 2 (Spring 1961): 158–181.

The role of the Communists in the UAW and Reuther's relations with them are examined in Bert Cochran, *Labor and Communism; The Conflict That Shaped American Unions* (Princeton, N.J.: Princeton University Press, 1977), which, despite its title, deals mainly with the auto workers; Roger Keeran, *The Communist Party and the Auto Workers Unions* (Bloomington: Indiana University Press, 1980); Harvey A. Levenstein, *Communism, Anticommunism, and the CIO* (Westport, Conn.: Greenwood Press, 1981); Philip Bonosky, *Brother Bill McKie: Building the Union at Ford* (New York: International Publishers, 1953), a rhapsodic account of a well-known Communist Ford worker; and William D. Andrew, "Factionalism and Anti-Communism: Ford Local 600," *Labor History* 20, no. 2 (Spring 1979): 227–255. The argument that Reuther was a dues-paying member of the Communist party for a time in the 1930s is advanced in Martin Glaberman, "A Note on Walter Reuther," *Radical America*, November–December 1973, pp. 113–117.

The union during and around World War II is dealt with in Barton J Bernstein, "The Automobile Industry and the Coming of the Second World War," *Southwestern Social Science Quarterly* 47, no. 1 (June 1966): 22–3; B. J. Bernstein, "Walter Reuther and the General Motors Strike of 1945–1946," *Michigan History* 49, no. 3 (September 1965): 260–277; Martin Glaberman, *Wartime Strikes; The Struggle Against the No-Strike Pledge in the UAW During World War II* (Detroit: Bewick Editions, 1980); Nelson N. Lichtenstein, "Industrial Unionism Under the No-Strike Pledge; A Study of the CIO During the Second World War," Ph.D. dissertation, University of California, Berkeley, 1974; N. N. Lichtenstein, "Auto

Worker Militancy and the Structure of Factory Life, 1937–1955," *Journal of American History* 67, no. 2 (September 1980); 335–353; N. N. Lichtenstein, "Ambiguous Legacy: The Union Security Problem During World War II," *Labor History* 18, no. 2 (Spring 1977): 214–238; and Joshua Freeman, "Delivering the Goods: Industrial Unionism During World War II," *Labor History* 19, no. 4 (Fall 1978): 570–593.

The history of the union and its black component is studied in the excellent volume by August Meier and Elliott Rudwick, *Black Detroit and the Rise of the UAW* (New York: Oxford University Press, 1979); and, for later periods, in Thomas R. Brooks, "Workers, Black and White: DRUMbeats in Detroit," *Dissent*, January–February 1970, pp. 16–25; and Brooks, "Black Upsurge in the Unions," *Dissent*, March–April 1970, pp. 124–134. See also James A. Geschwander, *Class, Race, and Worker Insurgency: The League of Revolutionary Black Workers* (Cambridge: Cambridge University Press, 1977).

Several postwar UAW topics are dealt with in Nancy Gabin, "Women Workers and the UAW in the Post–World War II Period: 1945–1954," *Labor History* 21, no. 1 (Winter 1979–1980): 5–30; A. W. Kornhauser, H. L. Sheppard, and A. J. Mayer, *When Labor Votes; A Study of Auto Workers* (New York: University Books, 1956); Jack W. Stieber, *Democracy and Public Review; An Analysis of the UAW Public Review Board* (Santa Barbara, Calif.: Center for the Study of Democratic Institutions, 1960); and Walter H. Uphoff, *Kohler on Strike: Thirty Years of Conflict* (Boston: Beacon Press, 1966).

Auto workers on the job and in their communities have been the subject of numerous sociological investigations. Among the more important are Bennett M. Berger, *Working-Class Suburb; A Study of Auto Workers in Suburbia* (Berkeley and Los Angeles: University of California Press, 1960); Robert Blauner, *Alienation and Freedom; The Factory Worker and His Industry* (Chicago: University of Chicago Press, 1964); Ely Chiney, *Automobile Workers and the American Dream* (Garden City, N.Y.: Doubleday, 1955); and Charles R. Walker and Robert H. Guest, *The Man on the Assembly Line* (Cambridge, Mass.: Harvard University Press, 1952). A selection of essays on recent problems in the workplace is in B. J. Widick, ed., *Auto Work and Its Discontents* (Baltimore and London: Johns Hopkins University Press, 1976).

For further reading on the history of workers and unions, the place to begin is David Brody, *Workers in Industrial America; Essays on the Twentieth Century Struggle* (New York: Oxford University Press, 1980). For the

Depression and the New Deal, see Irving Bernstein, *Turbulent Years; A History of the American Worker, 1933–1941* (Boston: Houghton Mifflin, 1970). Other general works include Thomas R. Brooks, *Picket Lines and Bargaining Tables; Organized Labor Comes of Age, 1935–1955* (New York: Grosset and Dunlap, 1968); and James R. Green, *The World of the Worker: Labor in Twentieth-Century America* (New York: Hill and Wang, 1980). Biographies of Reuther's labor contemporaries include Melvyn Dubofsky and Warren Van Tine, *John L. Lewis: A Biography* (New York: Quadrangle/New York Times, 1977); Joseph Goulden, *Meany* (New York: Atheneum, 1972); and Matthew Josephson, *Sidney Hillman: Statesman of Labor* (New York: Doubleday, 1952). On several other important topics, see Arthur J. Goldberg, *AFL-CIO: Labor United* (New York: McGraw-Hill, 1956); F. Ray Marshall, *The Negro and Organized Labor* (New York: Wiley, 1965); Joel Seidman, *Democracy in the Labor Movement*, 2nd ed. (Ithaca, N.Y.: New York State School of Industrial and Labor Relations, Cornell University, 1969); Sidney Lens, *The Crisis of American Labor* (New York: A. S. Barnes, 1961); Derek C. Bok and John T. Dunlop, *Labor and the American Community* (New York: Simon and Schuster, 1970); James C. Foster, *The Union Politic; The CIO Political Action Committee* (Columbia: University of Missouri Press, 1975); Jack Barbash, *The Practice of Unionism* (New York: Harper and Brothers, 1956) and *Labor's Grass Roots: A Study of the Local Union* (New York: Harper and Brothers, 1961); and Max M. Kampelman, *The Communist Party Versus the C.I.O.* (New York: Praeger, 1957). The Department of Labor's *Monthly Labor Review* provides useful accounts of many developments in unions and in collective bargaining.

For the history of the automobile industry John B. Rae, *The American Automobile: A Brief History* (Chicago: University of Chicago Press, 1965), offers an introduction. Gerald Bloomfield has written *The World Automoblie Industry* (North Pomfret, Vt.: David Charles, 1978), which contains useful material for recent years. The works of two economists—Lawrence J. White, *The Automobile Industry Since 1945* (Cambridge, Mass.: Harvard University Press, 1971); and Robert M. Macdonald, *Collective Bargaining in the Automobile Industry* (New Haven: Yale University Press, 1963)—are valuable. For an earlier period, the investigation of the Federal Trade Commission, *Report on the Motor Vehicle Industry* (Washington, D.C.: U.S. Government Printing Office, 1939), which concentrates on relationships between manufacturers and dealers, is still useful. For the 1920s see Robert W. Dunn, *Labor and*

Automobiles (New York: International Publishers, 1929). Of the manufacturers and their labor relations, only Ford Motor Company has received extensive historical treatment. The third volume of Allan Nevins's history of Ford, Allan Nevins and Frank Ernest Hill, *Ford: Decline and Rebirth, 1933–1962* (New York: Charles Scribner's Sons, 1963), covers the period of Reuther's activity; but see also the two earlier volumes for the most detailed available coverage of the industry's early years: Nevins, *Ford: The Times, the Man, the Company* (New York: Charles Scribner's Sons, 1954), and Nevins and Hill, *Ford: Expansion and Challenge, 1915–1933* (New York: Charles Scribner's Sons, 1957). A more critical work, which includes good accounts of Ford's labor relations, is Keith Sward, *The Legend of Henry Ford* (New York: Rinehart, 1948). The history of the employment of blacks in the industry may be studied in Lloyd H. Bailer, "Negro Labor in the Automobile Industry," Ph.D. dissertation, University of Michigan, 1943; and Herbert R. Northrup et al., *Negro Employment in Basic Industry; A Study of Racial Policies in Six Industries*, vol. 1: *Studies of Negro Employment* (Philadelphia: Wharton School of Finance and Commerce, University of Pennsylvania, 1970).

Among the many books on political issues, the following provided material on events in which Reuther was involved: Ralph S. Brown, Jr., *Loyalty and Security: Employment Tests in the United States* (New Haven: Yale University Press, 1958); David Caute, *The Great Fear* (New York: Simon and Schuster, 1978); Alonzo L. Hamby, *Beyond the New Deal: Harry S. Truman and American Liberalism* (New York and London: Columbia University Press, 1973); Joseph P. Lash, *Eleanor: The Years Alone* (New York: Norton, 1972); R. Alton Lee, *Truman and Taft-Hartley; A Question of Mandate* (Lexington: University of Kentucky Press, 1966); Mary S. McAuliffe, *Crisis on the Left; Cold War Politics and American Liberals, 1947–1954* (Amherst, Mass.: University of Massachusetts Press, 1978); Arthur M. Schlesinger, Jr., *Robert Kennedy and His Times*, 2 vols. (Boston: Houghton Mifflin, 1978); and Frank A. Warren, *An Alternative Vision: The Socialist Party in the 1930's* (Bloomington: Indiana University Press, 1974).

Index